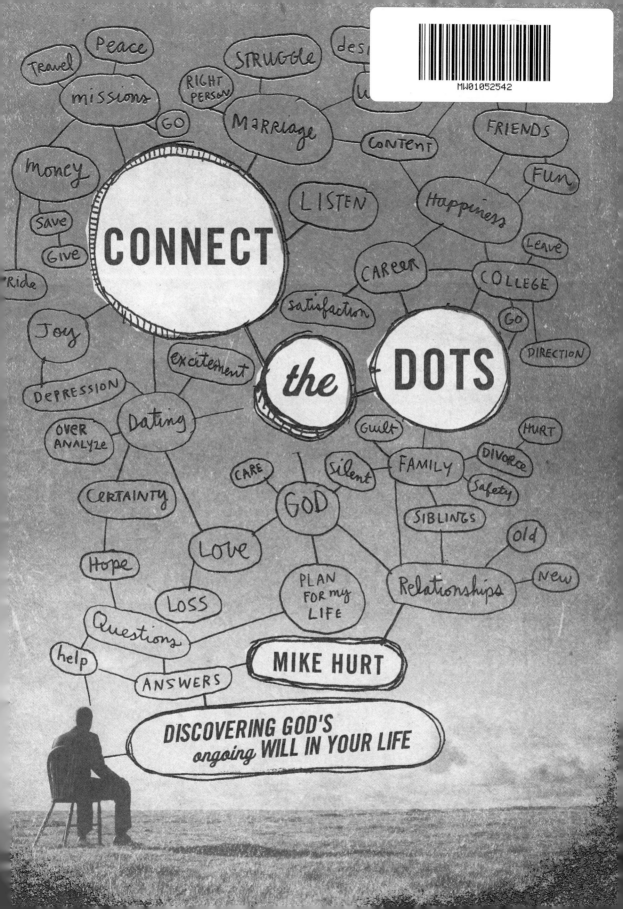

Published by LifeWay Press®
© 2007 LifeWay Press
Second Printing June 2008

No part of this work may be reproduced or transmitted in any form or by any means, electronic or mechanical, including photocopying and recording, or by any information storage or retrieval system, except as may be expressly permitted in writing by the publisher. Requests for permission should be addressed in writing to LifeWay Press®, One LifeWay Plaza, Nashville, TN 37234-0175.

ISBN: 978-1-4158-5730-4
Item Number: 005085765

Dewey Decimal Classification Number: 231.5
Subject Heading: GOD—WILL\ CHRISTIAN LIFE
Printed in the United States of America

Leadership Adult Publishing
LifeWay Church Resources
One LifeWay Plaza
Nashville, Tennessee 37234-0175

We believe the Bible has God for its author; salvation for its end; and truth, without any mixture of error, for its matter and that all Scripture is totally true and trustworthy. The 2000 statement of The Baptist Faith and Message is our doctrinal guideline.

Unless otherwise indicated, all Scripture quotations are taken from the Holman Christian Standard Bible® Copyright © 1999, 2000, 2002, 2003 by Holman Bible Publishers. Used by permission. Holman Christian Standard Bible®, Holman CSB®, and HCSB® are federally registered trademarks of Holman Bible Publishers. Scripture marked (NIV) is taken from the Holy Bible, New International Version, copyright © 1973, 1978, 1984 by International Bible Society.

TABLE of CONTENTS

Meet the Author

MIKE HURT

My name is Mike, and I'm an author, dad, husband, and pastor. I live in Victoria, Texas, with my wife, Kristi, and our three kids. Day in and day out, I have the unique opportunity to teach and to lead our church to thrive and impact lives and to make sure people are connecting with each other in real, biblical community. That's what really excites me— seeing people follow the Lord together. That idea has been formative in this study as well as my other study for Threads, *Repurposed: The Memoirs of Nehemiah.* Before moving to Victoria, I was on staff at McLean Bible Church and Frontline, just outside of Washington D.C. I was raised in Louisiana and then graduated with a Master of Divinity from Southwestern Baptist Theological Seminary.

I am convinced that to work hard you must play hard or maybe just watch a lot of TV. When I'm not working or catching up on all that TiVo® has to offer, I love to be outside, build relationships with my neighbors, and play with my kids. I am a confessed technology and e-mail addict.

It has been a very humbling process to write this book. To think that God would use me to help you know and live His will for your life amazes me. As you read and discuss *Connect the Dots,* I hope you find not just what you are looking for but what God has in store for you.

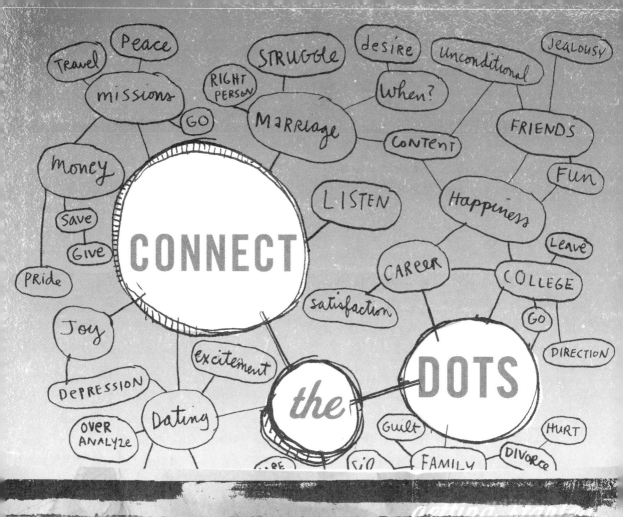

BEYOND THE BIG THREE

NOTHING SEEMS TO MOTIVATE A SEARCH FOR HIGHER PURPOSE THAN THE "BIG THREE." AS A PASTOR, I HAVE BEEN MEETING WITH YOUNG ADULTS FOR 15 YEARS. DURING THAT TIME, I HAVE LEARNED THAT THE BIG THREE . . .

WHO SHOULD I MARRY? WHERE SHOULD I WORK? AND WHERE SHOULD I LIVE?—CONSISTENTLY MOVE PEOPLE TO START ASKING THE SEEMINGLY SIMPLE QUESTION: "WHAT IS GOD'S WILL FOR MY LIFE?"

If you are asking these questions, you are certainly not alone—especially if you have spent a couple of years in the workplace and are wondering where you go from here. These are natural questions to ask; it's a part of growing in wisdom. It's a part of defining how you are going to live your life. It's a part of learning what it means to be you on your terms.

But perhaps that is also the flaw in the big three questions. It seems to me that we want to know God's will as long as His will lines up nicely with our ideas of what our lives should generally be like. That's usually why the big three prompt us to ask the question of God's will—we have in our minds and hearts what we want the answer to be. If that is true, then our question is not really, *What is God's will for my life?* Instead, it's, *Does God's will for my life line up with my vision for my life?*

The result is a jumbled blend of our ideas and God's ideas, our desires and His desires, our will and His will. Further complicating the situation is the reality that very few of us have ever seen the proverbial skywriting telling us exactly where to work or who to marry. Many more of us have asked for God to answer our big life questions, but at the end of the day, we have simply had to make a decision with little more than a sense of which direction God wants us to go. The search for any amount of certainty or confidence in God's will has become little more than a pipe dream for most of us. Like a carrot just out of reach of the horse's nose, we ask these big questions hoping to hear a cosmic voice affirm some direction, and yet that voice always seems to be just out of earshot.

Despite this, I firmly believe that God cares deeply about the big decisions of your life. Furthermore, I believe He is incredibly concerned about the mundane, ordinary moments of your life—so much so that perhaps the question God wants us to ask is slightly different than the one we are asking right now.

MAYBE, BECAUSE GOD WANTS TO BE INTIMATELY INVOLVED IN EVERY DETAIL OF YOUR LIFE, THE QUESTION YOU SHOULD BE ASKING IS NOT, *WHAT IS GOD'S WILL FOR MY LIFE?* BUT *WHAT IS GOD'S WILL IN MY LIFE?*

The difference is huge. If you are asking for God's will for your life, then you are looking for a crystal ball. You want to see into the future to try and find the most prosperous way to go. But if you recognize that God's will is not only *for* your life but *in* your life, then you are choosing to believe in a God who is more than just a fortune-teller. You are choosing to believe that God's greatest call is not for you to be married or single, a preacher or a doctor, to live in Miami or Beijing. His greatest call is for you to follow Jesus—every moment.

Maybe the next several weeks can be a time for you to rediscover that God doesn't just have a plan for you but that God cares deeply about you. Sometimes in the discussion of God's will, we can lose sight of God's love and kindness. If all we are looking for is God's will for our lives, then we betray our perception of God. Our questions reveal that we believe that God is very interested in what we do, where we go, and what we can accomplish on His behalf in the world. But is He only interested in us to the extent that we can be useful to Him?

But I believe God is much more interested in who we are than what we do. For this reason, we do not seek to find answers as much as we seek to find God Himself. It is only through our journey together with Him that we find answers, but amazingly, those answers will become of secondary importance to the great joy and satisfaction of just walking in relationship with God.

That's why it's so vital that we are convinced of God's love for us. Much in the same way that we do not just want answers from Him, He does not just want performance from us. We are meant for each other—us and God—and not just so that we can accomplish each other's desires. We are meant to walk with each other. We are meant to be in each other's lives. We are meant to live deeply together.

I hope that, for you, the end result of *Connect the Dots* is a greater love for, hope in, and commitment to the will of God in your life.

"GOD'S WILL IS MORE ABOUT US ANSWERING HIS QUESTIONS THAN HIM ANSWERING OURS."

Augustine, Bishop of Hippo, North Africa, was born to a pagan father and religious mother in 354. Though abandoning his Christian heritage as a teenager, he converted to Christianity in 386 and subsequently became, according to most, the most influential thinker and writer to Western Christianity other than Paul himself. Augustine died in 430.

THE NATURE OF GOD'S WILL

Sometimes the beginning of a spiritual journey is itself a journey. That seems to have been true of Augustine, Bishop of Hippo in North Africa. His mother prayed for him for years, but Augustine was reluctant to fully surrender himself to God and His will. He understood, even before he became a Christ-follower, that to undertake something like Christianity was to give yourself fully to it. Frankly, Augustine loved the world too much to do that.

Nevertheless, God won out, and over the subsequent years, Augustine became one of the greatest theological contributors to Western Christianity. In the *Confessions*, Augustine chronicled his journey to Jesus and the path that proceeded from his conversion. Indeed, his worst fears were true—that he had to fully give himself to the will of God if he were to have any relationship with Him at all. His journey reminds us that though many of us might ask to know God's will, very few of us are ready to fully embrace it:

> "I was troubled in spirit, most vehemently indignant that I entered not into Thy will and covenant, O my God, which all my bones cried out unto me to enter, and praised it to the skies. And therein we enter not by ships, or chariots, or feet, no, move not so far as I had come from the house to that place where we were sitting. For, not to go only, but to go in thither was nothing else but to will to go; but to will resolutely and thoroughly; not to turn and toss, this way and that, a maimed and half-divided will.

> "There is a joy which is not given to the ungodly, but to those who love Thee for Thine own sake, whose joy Thou Thyself art. And this is the happy life, to rejoice to Thee, of Thee, for Thee; this it is, and there is no other."[1]

THE NATURE OF GOD'S WILL

BEYOND THE BIG THREE

If God were a Magic 8 Ball, finding His will would be pretty easy—just a question, a shake, and an answer. But anyone who has asked and struggled with the big questions of life knows that it's not that simple. We ask our life questions; listen for a voice from heaven; look for signs in the circumstances around us; and then most of the time, we have to simply make a decision with some degree of uncertainty. The process is enough to drive us all crazy, because we all have really big questions that need really big answers.

The root of our questions might be what sociologists and psychologists call a "quarter-life crisis." In such a time, feelings of confusion about who you are and insecurities regarding the future can keep you up at night. Relational changes complicate things even further. You no longer live in the dorm, and the relationships that were so natural in your previous environment don't fit so well in your new 9 to 5, business-casual, ID-badge-wearing life. Throw in the financial stress you are feeling due to student loans, that new car you had to have, and that pair of jeans you put on the card years ago, and you have a crisis on your hands. What our parents experienced in their mid 40s, we are experiencing in our mid 20s.

You cannot live with this type of tension. If you combine financial stress, insecurity about the future, and relational disconnectedness, you will crash without a relationship with God. Even if you have a growing relationship with Christ, these can be some of the most challenging days of your life. That is why you come to an office like mine and talk to a pastor like me about issues like these: who you are going to marry, what you are supposed to do for a living, and where you should live—the big three. You come looking for God's will just as Tom did.

Tom, by all accounts, had it all. He was recent law school graduate. He had a job at a firm in the power center of the nation, Washington, D.C. He was in a small group, so he had solid friendships even though he was relatively new to the area. He even had the occasional date or two though there was nothing serious on the horizon. Despite "having it all," Tom had some serious questions about the direction of his life.

He came to my office to talk about one of the big three: his career. After a year or so on the job, he wasn't certain he wanted to practice law anymore, and if he was to continue practicing, he was sure that he was not going to practice the kind of law he had been since moving to D.C. There was nothing unethical or illegal happening; he just wasn't satisfied. So he popped the question: "What is God's will for me? What should I do with my life?"

I told Tom what I tell everyone else—you need to understand that God's will for your future is much more than just the answers to the big questions of your life. In fact, God's will is more about us answering His questions than Him answering ours. God can, and many times does, give us the answers we are looking for, but don't fool yourself—finding the answers to our big questions is not necessarily the same thing as discovering God's will for our lives. Though God wants us to come to Him for the answers that matter to us, He wants our full devotion more.

Think about this: If it were God's will for you to never discover the answers to the biggest questions of your life, would you still want to know God's will?

Fortunately, God does not choose to hide Himself from us. He is not playing some cosmic game of hide-and-seek when it comes to His will for our lives. A quick scan of the Old Testament shows that God's desire is to make Himself and His desires known. Probably the two most famous accounts that illustrate this both involve Moses—first at the burning bush in Exodus 3 and then at Mount Sinai in Exodus 34.

At the burning bush, Moses learned God's will for his life. He learned that God intended for Moses to lead His people out of captivity in Egypt. At Sinai, Moses learned God's will for Israel—and the rest of us for that matter—as he received the Ten Commandments. The New Testament also makes it clear that God wants to reveal Himself to us, for the person of Christ shows us who God really is.

Would you characterize your past experiences in finding God's will for your life as frustrating or encouraging? Why?

If God wants to reveal Himself to us, then why do you think it's so difficult to figure out His plan?

For further study on discovering God's will in a relational context, consider reading *God's Will, Our Dwelling Place* by Andrew Murray.

Download the *Connect the Dots* playlist.

Get the list from your group leader or at *www.threadsmedia.com/media*. Make it your soundtrack for this study.

FROM INQUIRY TO RELATIONSHIP

I believe we tend to think of God's will in one of three ways: as a formula, a connect-the-dots picture, or a relationship.

Many of us fall prey to thinking that God's will is the ultimate "if, then" formula: If I do this, then God will do that. The problem with this view is that God does not operate inside of formulas; He is bigger, wiser, and more powerful than that. We cannot be so arrogant as to assume that we can force God into a response by our acts of obedience.

Many others see God's will as a cosmic connect-the-dots picture. In such a picture, the goal is to draw an image by connecting the already-numbered points on the page. In just moments, the budding artist is able to draw perfect bears, flowers, or clown faces. We become artists simply because we can draw in the lines to complete the picture.

In a way, God's will *is* like connecting the dots because He has a plan and a future that He has designed specifically for us. But God's will is also very different from simply drawing in the lines. If you make a mistake while drawing connect-the-dots pictures, the whole picture is ruined and can never be completely fixed; you will always see the error. The same cannot be said of God's will. You can live God's will today no matter what you did yesterday. God can redeem and restore your life to His perfect plan at any point in time.

Rather than looking to equations or connect-the-dots experiences, God's will is best understood in the context of an intimate relationship. Consider the words Jesus used to describe people who were doing the will of the Father. In Mark 3:35, He said that the people who do His will are His brother and sister and mother. John 14:21 tells us that our obedience is a result of our love for God and His love for us. John 15:14 reminds us that we are His friends if we obey His commands.

Did you notice that none of these are mathematical terms? They are all relational terms. God wants us to discover and live out His will through a relationship with Him because at the core, God is relational. My mentor and friend Rich Hurst puts it this way: "Christianity offers intimacy with the God of the Bible, the God of creation, the God of history. Furthermore, the God of Christianity is a God who seeks us out. He wants to be intimate with us, and He pushes us to be known."[2] Don't miss the intimate invitation to a relationship with God as you discover His will.

Adopting a relational mind-set changes the way we pursue God's will for our lives. If we can find God's will best in a relational context, then our primary focus must be to develop the relationship and not just seek answers to our questions. Relationship development demands a high level of obedience, dedication, and discipline. Furthermore, these characteristics are not just important in developing a relationship; they are required because God expects us to take action once we know His will. He does not reveal Himself to us so that we know ourselves better; He reveals Himself to us so that we know Him better and can show our love for Him with the actions of our lives.

How does having a relational mind-set change the way you pursue God's will for your life?

Do you think most people approach God for answers or for a relationship? Why?

WHAT DIFFERENCE DOES IT MAKE?

What changes when you find God's will for your life? How would you live, work, relate, or worship differently than you did before you knew the will of God? You would agree that knowing does not always equal doing. Take the speed limit for example. We *know*, but we seldom *do*.

Some of us think that if we can find God's will for our lives we can put the controls on autopilot. In that mind-set, discovering the answers to our big questions means we don't have to work on the hard stuff anymore. We can become like the star of a well-traveled urban legend.

Perhaps an e-mail like this has cluttered your inbox:
"In November 2000, Mr. Grazinski purchased a brand new, 32-foot Winnebago motor home. On his first trip home, having joined the freeway, he set the cruise control at 70 mph and calmly left the drivers seat to go into the back and make himself a cup of coffee. Not surprisingly, the Winnie left the freeway, crashed, and overturned. Mr. Grazinski sued Winnebago for not advising him in the handbook that he could not actually do this. He was awarded $1,750,000 plus a new Winnebago."[3]

Listen to "What am I seeking?" before your group gets together to discuss this session. (Your group leader will send it to you via e-mail.)

Why do you want to know God's will? Is there an element of risk to the questions you are asking?

"Mr. Grazinski" apparently thought that cruise control meant autopilot. That's absurd to you and me; we know that to drive you need at least a knee on the wheel and a foot on the gas pedal. Don't become your own urban legend by thinking that God's will is like your personal autopilot. When you discover what God wants for you to do, it will take energy and effort on your part to live it out.

Many of us have the delusion that if we knew with certainty what God wanted us to do, then we would do it without question, no matter the cost. Not true—our personal history bears witness to it. There are commands in Scripture that you and I disobey every day. I don't know what your favorites are, but mine usually center on a rebellious attitude. Each of us can remember a time when we knew God wanted us to do something and we refused. His Spirit whispered to us, we knew it was God, and yet, we did not take action. Maybe it was a prompt to share your faith with a new friend or to shut your mouth when everyone else was bashing your boss. Whatever the instance, you ignored the prompting. You and I have proven it: Knowledge of God's will is no guarantee for obedience to God's will.

KNOWING AND DOING

Ironically, we find ourselves looking for the will of God while at the same time ignoring the will of God. We are not alone—some of the best-known men and women in Scripture have done the very same thing. Moses' first response at the burning bush was not obedience; it was hesitation. God told Moses what he should do in very clear terms. But instead of following God's instruction, Moses asked questions designed to let him off the hook.

What about Lot's wife in Genesis 19? She knew that judgment was coming on the city where her family was living. She also knew that she and her family were to be rescued by God because the Lord's messengers were working on their behalf and for their protection. Nevertheless, as she and her family were being rescued, she was disobedient. Rather than looking ahead to the place God was preparing for her, she looked back and became a part of the destruction that God was working to save her from. Knowing God's will did not give her the courage to leave everything.

I have heard people say that if they knew God was calling them to do so, they would leave everything and do whatever He wanted them to do, even if it was the most difficult task in the world. According to them, all they would need is the certainty of God's will, and they would go—no questions asked. Only a few have been able to keep this type of commitment. I think of a friend named Jason who left a job in the tech field and is now working to reach Muslims in South Hall, England.

I also think of Shannon who God gave a dream to lead people to rekindle their faith in Him. Shannon quit his job and is investing in people full-time and trusting God for the rest. These men have done what few of us do. They have let the will of God actually take root in their lives. Far more of us have chosen disobedience despite our knowledge of God's will.

One of the reasons certainty does not necessarily result in obedience is because God is not looking for certainty—He is looking for faith. While we want to know more, God wants us to trust more. While we want assurances concerning the future, God wants us to place our future in His hands. While we want our doubts and fears to go away, God wants to turn them into a strengthened faith in Him. It is our faith in the middle of every circumstance that pleases God—not our certainty of our next step.

God's Word is consistently clear that we will not discover God or His will for our lives without faith. Look at the contrast between the response of the Gentiles and Israel:

"What should we say then? Gentiles, who did not pursue righteousness, have obtained righteousness—namely the righteousness that comes from faith. But Israel, pursuing the law for righteousness, has not achieved the law. Why is that? Because they did not pursue it by faith, but as if it were by works. They stumbled over the stumbling stone" (Romans 9:30-32).

The Gentiles pursued God by faith and found what they were looking for. Israel pursued a law-based relationship with God rather than a faith-based relationship with God and came up short—way short. The lesson for us is clear: We must come to Christ by faith, pursue His will by faith, and live according to His plan for our lives by faith.

> Do you think God wants you to be absolutely certain of His specific will?

> Why or why not?

FAITH, NOT CERTAINTY

Isaiah should be our role model when it comes to discovering God's will for our lives. Isaiah was an eyewitness to a heavenly scene that cannot be rivaled by anything that you or I have ever seen on TV or a movie screen. He saw God sitting on His throne and His robe extended as far as the eye could see. Around God, there were heavenly creatures flying as they covered their eyes. The creatures revered God's holiness both with their posture and with their song: "Holy, holy, holy is the LORD of Hosts" (Isaiah 6:3). At their voices, the foundations of the temple shook.

Upon entering this scene, Isaiah immediately confessed his sin. Following his confession, one of the creatures grabbed a hot coal off the altar of the Lord and flew directly at Isaiah. The creature touched his lips with the hot coal and told him that his guilt had been removed and his sins atoned for. Then Isaiah heard the voice of the Lord asking who he should send and who would go out for the task at hand (Isaiah 6:1-8).

Before we get to Isaiah's response, I want you to imagine yourself in this scene. You have been invited to be a firsthand witness of God's glory. You see the throne and creatures. You hear the songs, and you respond appropriately by throwing yourself on the mercy of the Lord. Then your lips are touched with a hot coal to signify your forgiveness and purity. Now, standing before God, you are a new person. Then, you hear the voice of God. He clearly communicates His will through simple questions: "Whom shall I send? Who will go?" You know exactly what

God wants. The God who has forgiven you, cleansed you, and removed your guilt has shown you His will. You have no doubts. Would you respond as Isaiah did?

He responded with faith. No excuses. No looking back. He knew God's will and was willing to act on it in faith. His response was, "Here I am. Send me" (Isaiah 6:8). Did you notice that God did not tell Isaiah where He was sending him? Did you notice that God did not explain what Isaiah's role would be once he was sent? Did you notice that he did not know what he was supposed to say or do? Despite all these questions Isaiah could have asked, he responded with faith.

Once we understand the nature of God's will and that God's desire is for us to respond to Him with faith instead of certainty, we will find ourselves desiring a relationship with God that is lived through our intentional spiritual disciplines. It is then that the adventure of discovering and applying God's will for our lives begins. Enjoy the journey.

What is frightening to you about knowing God's will for your life?

The movie *Simon Birch* is a film centering on the question of whether or not God has a purpose for everyone's life. Just for a discussion starter, take a look at this movie with your group.

Do you think most people have a positive or negative outlook regarding the things God has for them in the future? Why?

THIS WEEK, BEGIN TO LET GOD REFORM YOUR UNDERSTANDING OF HIS WILL.

Consider Enoch in Genesis 5:24: "Enoch walked with God, and he was not there, because God took him." In Hebrew, the word *walk* indicates human movement but does not indicate a specific destination. It seems that Enoch was content to walk and let the answers about the future come when they came.

Make a list of all the big questions of your life you would love to have answered. Then spend some time each day committing the answers to the Lord and praying that you would value your present relationship with Him more than the answers He already knows.

Notes

2

"IF YOU SEARCH FOR GOD'S WILL WITHOUT EVER CONSULTING HIS WORD, YOU WILL NEVER FIND WHAT YOU ARE LOOKING FOR."

Madame Jeanne Guyon was born in 1648 at Montargis, France. At 15, she married into an unhappy union. Her husband—more than twice her age—was an invalid who needed her care. She sought happiness in her devotional life. Later she was imprisoned twice for her religious beliefs.

GOD'S WILL FOR EVERY DAY

During her life, Madame Jeanne Guyon was imprisoned more than once because of her religious fervor; in fact, almost 25 years of her life were spent in confinement. Most of her books were written during that time. In those works, Madame Guyon chronicled her own path to intimacy with Jesus and sought to instruct others on how to walk a similar road. One of the chief means for doing so was through the Word of God.

As you read Madam Guyon's writing, it becomes readily apparent that her "Bible reading" differs greatly from our own:

> "But in coming to the Lord by means of 'praying the Scripture,' you do not read quickly; you read very slowly. You do not move from one passage to another, not until you have *sensed* the very heart of what you have read. You may then want to take that portion of Scripture that has touched you and turn it into prayer . . . 'Praying the Scripture' is not judged by *how much* you read but the *way* you read. If you read quickly, it will benefit you little. You will be like a bee that merely skims the surface of a flower. Instead, in this new way of reading with prayer, you become as the bee who penetrates into the *depths* of the flower. You plunge deeply within to remove its deepest nectar."[4]

Plunge deeply. Drink fully. Depart slowly. And find in the pages the very words of God concerning His will for your life.

GOD'S WILL FOR EVERY DAY

HE HAS SPOKEN

Regardless of what anyone says, our society is hungry to know God's will. If you Google "God's will," your search will return several million results. Before you look for the proverbial needle of truth in a haystack of untested Web content, you need to know the first place you should look to truly discover the will of God. If you know this, you can discover God's will for your life every day. Really, you can.

God has made His will for every day of our lives clear. You can know what to do every day. You can know how to think every day. You can know how to relate to people every day. You can know what God wants for you every day. So where do you find this wealth of knowledge? The answer to this question is simpler than you think. God's Word, the Bible, is the where we find His will for every day of our lives.

The Bible is a blend of God's story, commands, and instructions to His followers. All of Scripture is intended to communicate God's desires, will, and plan for the world. Because of this, reading, knowing, studying, and applying God's Word is central to discovering God's will for every day of your life.

Second Timothy 3:16-17 outlines three reasons that we should look to Scripture as our first and primary source for discovering God's will:

"All Scripture is inspired by God and is profitable for teaching, for rebuking, for correcting, for training in righteousness, so that the man of God may be complete, equipped for every good work."

To say that Scripture is God-breathed is to claim its absolute uniqueness. The Bible has God as its author, and as He inspired men to record His activity, He revealed His will for the way we should live our lives. Have a question, concern, need, or desire? Check it against God's Word. The Bible reveals what God continues to desire from His people. Those Holy Scriptures clearly teach us when we are lacking knowledge, rebuke and correct us when necessary, train us to become more like Christ in our day-to-day lives, and prepare us for every good work.

Listen to "Has God already spoken?" before your group gets together to discuss this session. (Your group leader will send it to you via e-mail.)

Think about whether or not your questions take into account what God has already said.

DON'T FORGET YOUR BIBLE

If it is true that the Word of God is the ultimate source of truth for our lives, why is it that many times it is the last place we check when we look for direction? Think about the last time you were looking for God's specific will in your life. What did you do? Maybe you were looking for direction concerning a relationship, so you went to the relationship section of a local bookstore. Here you found a myriad of relationship resources, but the advice recorded there seemed incomplete and not fully satisfying. Perhaps it felt like that because it was *advice*. While those books may have elements of truth in them, advice cannot ultimately change your life or answer your deepest questions.

It's much easier to let others do the hard work for us. Rather than searching the Bible on our own, we look to others for their take on our situation. If we aren't careful, we will be more committed to authors than "the author and perfecter of our faith" (Hebrews 12:2, NIV). After all, John Ortberg is a great writer, but if you quote him more than you quote Jesus Christ, there is a problem.

Books, friends, and pastors are all helpful in discerning God's plan; I am not suggesting that you search for God's will in a vacuum. But if you search for His will without ever consulting His Word, you'll never find what you are looking for. You are looking for what only Scripture can provide: a word from the Lord. Second Peter 1:21 reminds us:

" . . . no prophecy ever came by the will of man; instead, moved by the Holy Spirit, men spoke from God."

The Word of God is like no other source in our world. It is authored by God with men as His writing instrument in order to communicate His message for all generations. These human pencils did not write their own words or opinions; they spoke for God as His Spirit worked in their lives. Because of this, the Bible is our first source for discovering God's will in our lives. God's Word tells us what God's moral will is, and it also gives us principles that serve as spiritual parameters needed to live a God honoring life.

> Why do you think more people don't look to the Bible for the will of God?

What needs to change in your treatment of Scripture for you to use it as God intended?

THE WORDS OF MEN AND THE WORD OF GOD

Why do we look to the words of men when we really need the words of God? In my experience, there are a couple of reasons we are reluctant to look to God's Word as our first source to discover His will, and they represent two ends of the biblical-confidence continuum.

Some among us don't consult God's Word because we have a "been there; done that" attitude when it comes to Scripture. Let me describe a person like this. He was most likely raised in church. Throughout his life, he has been involved in Sunday School, youth groups, and probably a Bible study on campus when he went to college. He has been saturated with study, but something went wrong along the way. As a teenager, he had real questions about God, but rather than talking, he kept quiet and joined everyone else in playing the junior high games.

Without a solid foundation of God's Word, he soon began to struggle with sin issues as he experienced new levels of freedom and choice. Rather than turning to the Bible for answers, he began to live as though God's Word was just like the books he was reading in English class—no study, no interaction, and no real application. Over time, he developed the perception that he had read everything the Bible has to offer, and that there is little to be found in its pages that deals with real life.

The other end of the spectrum represents those among us who are scared to study God's Word on our own. While this person is confident in the Bible, she is not confident in herself. She believes that Scripture does speak into the details of her life, but she feels ill equipped to find answers in its words.

Among the many resources about how to study the Bible, *Living by the Book* by Howard Hendricks is one of the best. This book will benefit the new student and the biblical scholar alike.

If this is you, I recommend you do a couple of things. First, develop a habit of reading God's Word consistently. When I came to know Christ, I read the book of 1 John every night for a month. As I read each day, I grew in confidence and understanding of the Bible. Before long, I began to see real answers for my questions about life. I found myself able to go to the Bible and find the truth that mattered in specific situations. It is possible, by the power of God's Spirit in your life, to read, understand, and apply scriptural truth to your life.

So what should you look for as you try to discover God's will through His Word? Look first for the direct commands in Scripture. There are literally hundreds of commands in the Bible that are without question God's will for your life because they are God's will for everyone's life!

Take a look at this short list of things God notes as His will:

1. It is God's will that I avoid sexual immorality (1 Thessalonians 4:3-8).

2. It is God's will that I rejoice always (1 Thessalonians 5:16).

3. It is God's will that I pray constantly (1 Thessalonians 5:17).

4. It is God's will that I give thanks in all circumstances (1 Thessalonians 5:18).

5. It is God's will that I submit to governing authorities (1 Peter 2:13-15).

God's will is clear in these passages. If you are looking for God's will right now, start with the clear commands in Scripture.

> What kinds of things prevent you from finding real life answers in the Bible?

> In what ways are you living according to God's general will? What ways are you lacking?

MORE SPECIFICALLY . . .

Knowing the Lord's clear commands will help us know generally how to live, but we still may be left with nagging questions about what God wants us to do in specific circumstances. Don't worry—the Bible has the solution for this, too. Psalm 119 is one of the most gut-level, honest passages in all of Scripture. If you didn't know that it is an acrostic poem, you would think it was the blog of a current day Christ-follower because of the struggle penned there.

The psalm flows from times of celebration to times of sadness and grief and continues through statements of great confidence in God. It is the strangest blend of desperation and hope. I think the psalmist knew what we should all learn: While I may have doubts, concerns, and fears about my life, I have no doubts, concerns, or fears about God's Word. It can be fully trusted.

Back to the big three—dating, work, and residence. God's Word will not tell us the name of the person we should date. The Bible won't tell us specifically where to work or even where to live. It will, however, instruct us on what a godly relationship looks like, who we should be at work, and the quality of the homes we are to build. God's Word builds us into people of character and hope as we discover His specific will for our lives.

Fully trusting God's Word should be one of our life goals. We should long for our souls to echo the psalmist as he wrote:

"I am continually overcome by longing for Your judgments" (Psalm 119:20).

"Your decrees are my delight and my counselors" (Psalm 119:24).

"Help me stay on the path of Your commands, for I take pleasure in it" (Psalm 119:35).

"I thought about my ways and turned my steps back to Your decrees" (Psalm 119:59).

"I will never forget Your precepts, for You have given me life through them" (Psalm 119:93).

With that level of commitment, we can all develop disciplines that will lead us to discover God's will through Scripture.

What are some practical ways you can begin to *love* the Bible?

How do you think a mature believer transfers the framework of decision-making to the specific decisions in his or her life?

DISCIPLINE

The first discipline we must develop is **consistent reading** of Scripture. Before we know the specifics of our dating lives, we need a cover-to-cover relationship with the Word of God. For us to discover the will of God in every area of our lives, we must consider the whole counsel of God's Word. I'm not suggesting that you read the Bible through every day. Even if that were possible, it would not be a healthy practice. What I am suggesting is that you develop a consistent reading plan.

You may want to adopt a plan to read the Bible in a year. You would be surprised how much you can read in 20 minutes a day. Or you may want to commit to read the books of the Bible that you haven't read yet. Whatever the plan, get in the Bible consistently and God will begin to show you His will in ways and places like never before.

I'm one of the few people in the world who actually reads the owner's manual for my car. I read it cover to cover. Even though I normally don't enjoy reading instructions, something comes over me when I see that particular booklet. I have read the manuals within hours of purchasing my last two vehicles. I find it so intoxicating that I will even read the owner's manual of rental cars. I can't resist. There is a part of me that wants to be able to utilize every feature of the vehicle. So I read, and I learn how to maximize my driving experience. We all need this type of discipline when it comes to reading God's Word.

To get a plan for consistent Bible reading, visit *www. backtothebible.org.*

There you can find reading plans based on chronology, history, blend of Old and New Testament, and more.

The second discipline is **study**. Along with simply reading, we should be studying as well. Choosing what to study depends on a few things. If you are studying the Bible in a group with other people, you should study what they are studying. It sounds like a given, but sometimes we can stretch ourselves too thin. It's hard to really study more than one passage at a time with great depth. So if you are in a group, study along with the group. Outside of group experiences, you should study the passages that are most confusing, exciting, or bring the most questions to mind as you execute your reading plan.

The proper study of God's Word leads us to the third discipline that God uses to show us His will through Scripture: **meditation**. For me personally, meditation is a key spiritual discipline for discovering God's will from His Word. Unfortunately, many times people get caught up on the word *meditation*. It's too mystical. They fear that it is the slippery slope to practicing eastern religions that have no connection to Christianity. Despite these objections, we are commanded to meditate:

"This book of instruction must not depart from your mouth; you are to recite it day and night, so that you may carefully observe everything written in it" (Joshua 1:8a).

Psalm 1:2 tells us that the man who meditates on God's law day and night will be blessed. Eight times in Psalm 119 alone we read references to meditation on the Word of God. It is clear from Scripture that there is nothing to fear in meditation as long as God and God's Word are the focus.

I think a lot of the confusion regarding this practice can be cleared up with a more accurate understanding of what meditation actually is. You don't have to do yoga to meditate; in fact, *meditation* is defined as: "continuous and profound contemplation or musing on a subject or series of subjects of a deep or abstruse nature."[5] Meditation is nothing strange; it's just some serious thought focused on God's Word. Dallas Willard describes it like this:

> "We not only read, hear, and inquire, but we meditate on what comes before us; that is, we withdraw into silence where we prayerfully and steadily focus upon it. In this way, its meaning can emerge for us and from us as God works in the depths of our heart, mind and soul."[6]

Listen to "I Still Haven't Found What I'm Looking For" by U2 on your playlist.

Could it be that we are looking in the wrong place for God's will?

For me, meditating means that I read a verse or a short passage and think about it over and over again. I think about it in different settings. I think about it when I am with people and when I am alone. I do everything I can to focus on that passage until I feel as though God has taught me what I am to learn through it. Without meditating on the Word of God, my reading would become a contest in speed, and my study would become a purely intellectual exercise. Meditation forces me to slow down and to chew on every morsel from the text.

When I am looking for God's will in my life regarding a particular situation, I meditate often, and people don't even know it. I live the very same pattern that I am suggesting to you: read, study, and meditate. I read so that I know God's Word, I study so that I understand God's Word, and I meditate so that I ingest and apply God's Word. Reading, studying, and meditating on God's Word is the first step in discovering God's will for your life. Through these three disciplines God will show you what He wants you to do every day.

When you think about discovering God's will, what matters more to you? Are you looking to know God's will for every day of your life or just on the days, weeks, or months that you have big questions or decisions to make? If you choose the latter, realize that *every day* matters more to God than the "big" days. Before you ask God about the details of your life, build your life on the principles, commands, and examples that you find in Scripture. As you do this, you will find the answers for every day that you are looking for.

How can you make more room in your life for meditation?

What is the difference in finding God's will for every day and finding His will for specific decisions you must make?

"REMEMBER TO DEDICATE THE SABBATH DAY . . ." THERE MAY BE NOTHING ELSE QUITE AS NEGLECTED IN OUR LIVES TODAY AS *SABBATH.* In a country that prizes busyness and productivity, the idea of *stopping* is useless. Maybe that is part of the mystery of Sabbath. The noun means an intermission; the verb means to cease and desist, to stop. But the true beauty of Sabbath is not just in the rest that happens when we stop—it's in the reflection that is meant to take place during that rest.

God was the first one to introduce this practice, and He did so not because He was tired; He stopped because He wanted to reflect and celebrate what He had accomplished. This coming Sabbath day, don't plan out your week. Don't go to the movies. Don't pay your bills. Rather, follow the Lord's example and reflect. Reflect on what the Lord has taught you this week. Journal about your experiences. Don't concern yourself with the challenges of tomorrow, but cease and enjoy the work of God in your life over the past several days.

Notes

3

"GOD IS AT WORK IN EVERY SITUATION AND IS TEACHING US WHAT HE WANTS US TO DO AS WE WALK THROUGH LIFE WITH HIM."

Born Gerrit Gerritszoon in Rotterdam, Holland, in 1646, Erasmus was almost certainly an illegitimate child. He took monastic vows reluctantly at age 25, though he spent his life attacking what he saw as excesses in the church. Erasmus worked to bring "religion" to the people, working for reformation and calling for translations of the Bible into popular languages.

GOD'S WILL IN ALL SEASONS

From the outside looking in, the idea that there is a single Being in the universe who is powerful enough—or arrogant enough in some people's minds—to presume to have a plan for every other being in the universe, amounts to little more than magic or superstition. Christ-followers affirm the truth that the Almighty does indeed have a plan but add that His plan is one of love for His creation. We counter the superstitious assumptions, but many of us seek to find God's will in superstitious ways:

"If a blue bird lands on my car during lunch . . ."

"If a particular song comes on the radio . . ."

"If she turns and looks at me . . ."

Surely God has a better way than these "tests" for us to know His will.

Erasmus (1469-1536) of Rotterdam, Holland, thought so. Called the prince of Christian humanists, Erasmus was a champion of common sense and intelligence. Much to the contrary of superstitious systems, he cared for practical Christianity and real-life ethics. In his *Handbook of a Christian Soldier,* Erasmus argued: "Whether it be through negligence or ignorance, most Christians are superstitious instead of pious and except for the name of Christ are not far from the superstition of the heathen."[7]

If we are to seek God's will with depth and maturity, we must move past the superstitious quick fixes and into the hard work of seeking the Lord . . .

GOD'S WILL IN ALL SEASONS

PROVIDENCE

God wants us to know His will each day of our lives. He is at work in every situation and is teaching us what He wants us to do as we walk through life with Him. It amazes me that God can teach me through the ordinary circumstances of my life, and it blows me away to think that He is doing that same thing in the life of every Christ-follower walking the planet today.

If we are going to find God's will in our daily lives, we must come to believe a couple of truths. First of all, we must be convinced that God is in control of the world in which we live. Secondly, we must believe that we can discern His will by watching His activity around us.

Discovering God's will through your day-to-day circumstances starts with realizing that God is in charge. Since He is in charge, He can teach us and speak to us through the otherwise normal activities of our lives. Theologians use the term *providence* to describe this reality:

> "Providence is in certain ways central to the conduct of the Christian's life. It means that we are able to live in the assurance that God is present and active in our lives. We are in his care and can therefore face the future confidently, knowing that things are not happening merely by chance."[8]

Millard Erikson's definition of providence gives us a picture of a relational God who is actively involved in both human activity and nature as a whole. We can find God's will through our day-to-day lives because God is intimately involved in the world around us.

God could have chosen for you to be born any time, at any place on the globe, and yet He chose *right here, right now*. For me, not only did God choose the 21st century, but He chose Washington, D.C., in the 21st century. Just as God has placed me in D.C., He has placed you where you are now. None of us are where we are by accident. I love the way Acts 17:26 puts it:

"From one man He has made every nation of men to live all over the earth and has determined their appointed times and the boundaries of where they live . . ."

Right now, God has you where you are for a reason. Six years ago, it was not my choice to move from South Texas to D.C.—it was God's design.

As we accept God's control of our circumstances, we must also accept His continual movement in the world around us. The question is not whether or not God is busy throughout the world; the question is how aware we are going to be of His ongoing work:

> "Because God's sovereign plan *will* be done, it isn't up to us to consciously bring it about. However, by being aware of how God is at work, we have clues about how to make decisions. We also grow in our faith as we see plans fall together that we have presented to Him, and we learn to relax in His control in our lives."[9]

As we live our day-to-day lives, we must actively look for God's activity around us. If we seek a high level of sensitivity to the work of God around us, we will begin to see His hand everywhere.

It's kind of like when you get a new car. You probably took little notice of that type of car before you bought it, but the moment that you drove off the lot, you started to see car after car just like the one you were steering. *You see what you are looking for.* It's true with cars, and it's true with God. If you are looking for His activity, you will notice it in places that you never have before.

How can you develop vision for God's ongoing activity in the world?

What does it mean to "practice the presence of God"?

Listen to "Burning Bushes" by Andy Gullahorn on your playlist.

What are your burning bushes? Does God still use signs like that?

THE OPEN DOOR

One common, but potentially dangerous, way we look for God's will in circumstances is by looking for the "open door." We have questions about decisions we need to make, and when it is not clear what we should do, we begin to hope and pray for God to "open and close doors." By this statement, we mean that God should provide a clear path to the opportunity He has for us and place immovable obstacles in the way of the paths we should avoid. This is the purest form of circumstantial evidence—if the option remains, it must be from God. While this sounds good at first, it makes the dangerous assumption that every opportunity put before you is God's opportunity for you.

First Samuel 24:3-7 is a great example of how every "open door" is *not* necessarily God's will for our lives. Saul and 3,000 of his men were pursuing David in order to kill him. While on the chase, Saul desperately needed to make a pit stop. Little did he know, David and his men were already in the cave where Saul chose to relieve himself. David had the opportunity to kill the king. If he did so, he easily could have taken over the throne.

Though God had promised David that he would rule Israel, David knew his rise to power was not to come about through murder. So instead of taking the king's life, David cut off a piece of Saul's robe as a sign of what could have been. Though he had only ripped the king's clothing, David later regretted his action and was so grief-stricken that he forbade his men from hurting the king in any way. He learned an abiding lesson that day: Every opportunity is not God's opportunity. Sometimes we must make decisions based on what we know of God rather than just what we see as a golden opportunity.

We know both from experience and Scripture that some options before us are not God's choice for us. These are situations where an "open door" leads to sin. Before you walk through a door thinking that God has opened it for you, take a peek through it and consider what this opportunity will do for your character and ability to obediently follow Christ. If taking the opportunity compromises either of these two things, then turn around; it is not a door that God has opened for you.

So how do you know if you are walking through God's door for you? Look for God's activity rather than just an open door. Consider how the apostle Paul made a decision about when and where he would minister. First Corinthians 16:9 reveals Paul stayed in Ephesus because of a wide open door but not just a wide open door. He stayed "because a wide door for *effective ministry*" opened for him *(emphasis added)*. Paul stayed not simply because he could, but because God's activity in Ephesus was so clear. In light of what God was doing there, he had no option but to stay. Since his motive and message were pure, he could confidently walk through the door the Lord opened. The lesson from Paul's ministry and prayer life is clear: When looking for God's will, don't just look for opportunities to come and go. Look for God's activity and go where He is at work.

THE EASY WAY OUT

Another misconception of discovering God's will through everyday life is found in one of the most misquoted Scriptures in the entire Bible:

"We know that all things work together for the good of those who love God: those who are called according to His purpose" (Romans 8:28).

To use the 90s phrase, many see this as the "it's all good" verse of the Bible. If I apply this verse out of context, I will always look for the easy way out of difficult situations or decisions because it is God's will to make everything good for me. The problem with this is that we have the misconception that *good* means *comfortable*.

If we look at the surrounding verses, however, we see the fallacy in that definition. Those verses do not promise that everything ends up easy and comfortable for us. Instead, the verses teach that in all things, God conforms us to the likeness of His Son. That's what is ultimately good—it's not about us and our comfort; it's about being conformed to the character of Jesus Christ.

The full context of Romans 8:28 blows up the idea that God's goal is to make us comfortable, but it also does something else—it gives us hope. If I think everything is supposed to be "good" in my eyes and I find myself in difficult circumstances, I will wonder if God is at work. If I think that God is not working, then how can I persevere? But if I know that God works as He pleases in every circumstance in life, then I can see His activity in everything. Because I know He is always at work, I can have the courage to make difficult decisions and take risks when He leads.

Brother Lawrence wrote about the moment-by-moment discovery of the will of God, even through tasks as menial as washing dishes. His book, *The Practice of the Presence of God*, remains classic instruction for Christ-followers.

There will be times in your life when God wants you to take the hard road rather than the easy one. He will call you to times of sacrifice. He will call you to times of risk. He will call you to times of pain and despair. But you can walk confidently with Christ through these times because you believe God is working all the time toward His ultimate will for your life—being conformed to the character of Jesus.

> How have you used the "open door" theory to find God's will in the past?

> How, if ever, have you misinterpreted Romans 8:28 in regard to God's will?

Listen to "Am I just waiting for the future?" before your group gets together to discuss this session. (Your group leader will send it to you via e-mail.)

How can you engage with God in the present rather than just waiting for the future?

TWENTY-FIRST CENTURY FLEECES

Another way that we look for God's will is through fleeces. We learn the principle of the fleece through God's interaction with Gideon (Judges 6). An angel of the Lord visited Gideon and told him that he was going to lead his people to defeat their oppressors, the Midianites. Gideon knew God's will, but he had questions. Gideon's solution to his doubt was to ask God for a sign. So he made a deal with God. Gideon would put a wool fleece out on the ground overnight. If, in the morning, the fleece was wet but the ground around it was dry, then God's will would be confirmed.

Gideon woke to find that the fleece was so wet that he wrung a bowlful of dew out of it. But, in yet another example of how certainty is no guarantee for obedience, Gideon made another request of God. This sign also involved a fleece, but this time Gideon wanted the fleece to be dry and the ground around it covered with dew. That night, God did exactly as Gideon requested. Apparently, two signs from God were enough for Gideon; he took action and conquered the Midianites as promised.

Following Gideon's example, we put out our own 21st century fleeces:

> God, if You want me to take that job, let the salary be $10,000 more
> than I make today.

> God, if You want me to date that person, let him come up and talk
> to me.

> God, if You want me to serve in ministry, bring someone across my
> path who gives me an opportunity in the next two weeks.

When I see the way Jesus responded to the religious crowd of His day, I am hesitant to use the fleece as a means for discovering God's will in my life. Just after Jesus fed 4,000 people with little more than you and I eat for lunch, He was questioned by a group of Pharisees. They requested a sign from heaven. After all, He had just fed 4,000 people, so surely He would give them a simple sign. Notice how Jesus responded:

"But sighing deeply in His spirit, He said, 'Why does this generation demand a sign? I assure you: No sign will be given to this generation!'" (Mark 8:12).

Why would no sign be given? We find the answer in John 4:48:

"'Unless you people see miraculous signs and wonders,' Jesus told him, 'you will never believe.'"

When Jesus walked the earth, He was not a first century David Blaine. He was not on the earth to entertain people with street-side miracles and magic tricks. He walked among us so that we would learn to love Him, trust Him, and give our lives to Him by faith. Signs don't always lead to obedience, and Jesus knew it.

What signs have you asked God for in your life?

Is it wrong to ask for signs?

COMMON SENSE IS NOT YOUR ENEMY

Don't check your brain at the door when looking for God's perspective on your day-to-day life. If God is at work in you and renewing your mind, common sense is not your enemy. In fact, as God renews your mind, you will actually be able to test and approve God's will (Romans 12:1-2). Unfortunately, some of us will never be able to confidently discern God's will through our everyday circumstances because we don't trust ourselves to make the right choice. Part of maturing in Christ, however, is being willing to responsibly accept the freedom to choose what God has given us. *Choice* is a part of God's plan for your life:

> "God's sovereignty decreed that man should be free to exercise moral choice, and man from the beginning has fulfilled that decree by making his choice between good and evil. When he chooses to do evil, he does not thereby countervail the sovereign will of God but fulfills it, in as much as the eternal decree decided not which choice the man should make but that he should be free to make it."[10]

We see this pattern in the creation account in Genesis 1-3. Think about all the choices Adam got to make concerning the world around him. Adam had the freedom to be fruitful and multiply. He was given the authority to subdue the earth. He was to rule over all of God's creation—the birds, fish, livestock, and even the insects, snakes, and other creatures that move along the ground. He was allowed to name all of the animals. He was given every plant and tree for food. God even created the institution of marriage for Adam as He gave Eve to Adam and Adam to Eve.

God gave Adam ultimate freedom to make wise decisions. Essentially, He said to Adam, "Enjoy everything that I have created for you. The only thing I ask is that you not eat from the tree in the middle of the garden. Stay clear of the tree of the knowledge of good and evil. Other than that, enjoy My creation." You probably know the rest of the story. Under the influence of one crafty serpent, Adam and Eve both ate from the tree in the middle of garden. As they ate that forbidden fruit, the world they lived in—and subsequently, the world we live in—was turned on its head. Instead of experiencing the freedom God designed for them, they experienced His discipline as they were booted from the garden of Eden. No longer would their life be marked by the simple enjoyment of God's creation; it would be characterized instead by labor, toil, and pain.

So what is the lesson that we can learn from God's dealings with Adam and Eve? First, God's perfect design includes room for people to make significant decisions. Second, even though God gives us generous freedom, there are limits. Just as God's boundaries were clear with Adam and Eve, His boundaries are clear with us. Third, if we are making decisions and living our lives consistently with His clear commands, we can move forward knowing that we are in line with God's will for our lives.

How do your choices and God's sovereignty work together?

What would make you confident in your ability to make major decisions?

GOD'S WILL ON THE GOOD DAYS

This may seem counterintuitive, but discovering God's will on the good days may be more difficult than discovering God's will on the difficult days. There are times when things just seem to click—when everything seems right with the world. At work, everything we touch turns to gold. Our relationships with friends and family are great. All around, things could not be any better. You would think that these should be the easiest times to discover what God wants, right? Wrong. In the good times, we don't often turn to God and ask for help, direction, or insight. Why do we need God when things are good? While we would never state that verbally, we consistently reveal this attitude with our lives.

On the good days, we need to passionately pursue God's will so that we are certain we are living His plan and not our own. Remember, God's will is much larger than just your happiness. If we build a life that centers on ourselves, then we never ask God what He wants us to do in the good times. We simply keep on living. Practically, this works until good days start to end and bad days begin.

The good days are not just times when we coast through life; they are times of preparation. God wants you to learn to trust and depend on Him when times are good so that in every circumstance you can express the same confidence in God's ongoing work in your life. If you are blessed enough to be in the middle of a good season of life right now, ask yourself this question: *Am I pursuing God's will in my life with the same level of passion I would if my life were in the dumps and I could barely survive?* If the answer is *no,* then you are failing to learn the truths that will pull you through the difficulties that are inevitably coming.

GOD'S WILL ON THE DIFFICULT DAYS

God uses the good and the bad circumstances of our lives to show us His will. I have already touched on the idea that God uses difficult circumstances to bring about His ultimate will for our lives—to make us more like Christ. In His power, God uses the trials and temptations that we experience to make us more like Him. James 1:4 encourages us to consider the difficult times in our lives as joy because these times of testing produce perseverance. This Spirit-enabled perseverance leads to maturity.

The next time you are in the middle of a difficult circumstance and find yourself asking, *Why me?,* realize that God is at work in your situation. He is in charge. As you realize this and know that you can trust Him, the question will begin to change from *God, why me?* to *God, what do You want to do in me?*

Difficult circumstances can also show us that it is God's will to use us to care for others. Second Corinthians 1:3-5 teaches us that we can extend the comfort we have received from God to other people in pain. God's love, compassion, and understanding can overflow through us into the circumstances of others. This is how God redeems even the most difficult situations of our lives. The way God reached you may very well be how He wants you to reach others. Your past pain could be your future ministry.

In our church, we have a number of ministries that were started by people as a way of sharing God's comfort with others just as He shared it with them. One that stands out to me is the Hope Cancer Ministry. This ministry is led by people who have been personally affected by cancer. They all have a heart for sharing God's love, hope, and encouragement with cancer patients and their families. This team has seen God faithfully bring them through one of the scariest times in their lives, and they have responded with ministry. Because they know what it means to experience God's comfort, they have committed to sharing that same comfort with others.

We should all look at the difficult circumstances we are facing or have faced and ask the question, *When will God use my past to reach someone for Christ?* This puts a whole different perspective on pain and God's redeeming power. He can use every piece of your life, because through Christ's death on the cross, every part of you has been forgiven and made new.

Take a few moments and reflect on how much worry there is in your life. What inner need or expectation does your worry reflect? Write about it.

Do you think it's easier to find the will of God on the good or the bad days? Why?

Why is it difficult to accept that God is in control during difficult circumstances?

WORRY

The Bible teaches us that God provides for all of our needs in every circumstance of our lives. God's provision helps us to overcome the main obstacle we face in finding God's will through our daily circumstances: worry.

Jesus taught that trusting God's provision is the only solution to the worry in our lives. He drew on pictures from nature—the birds of the air and the lilies of the field. The birds don't store up seed, yet they eat. The lilies don't labor, yet they are clothed more beautifully than history's richest man, Solomon. Rather than worrying about the things we need (or think we need), we should seek God and His kingdom. He knows our needs and will provide for us in every circumstance. Jesus concluded that we should not worry about tomorrow because today has enough troubles of its own (Matthew 6:25-34). If we don't hear the words of Jesus regarding God's provision, we will worry through our circumstances rather than learn from them.

"Don't worry about anything, but in everything, through prayer and petition with thanksgiving, let your requests be made known to God. And the peace of God, which surpasses every thought, will guard your hearts and your minds in Christ Jesus" (Philippians 4:6-7).

In order to overcome worry and live a life that sees God in the everyday circumstances of life, we must learn to live a life of disciplined prayer. Maybe it's a no-brainer, but I think it needs to be said: If you are seeking God's will without prayer, you will never find it. It's through prayer that God both gives us peace and reveals His will to us. Peace comes and worry departs as we present our requests to God with an attitude of thanksgiving (Philippians 4:6-7). This is no ordinary peace. It's a peace that is unexplainable and indescribable. It surpasses all understanding.

To experience this peace through prayer, develop an ongoing conversation with God throughout your day. It's possible even in the fast paced, multi-tasking, gotta-meet-a-deadline world that we live in to pray consistently throughout your day. You can pray when you wake up that God will bless your day and that you will honor Him. You can pray as you drive to work or to school. Think through your day and ask God to guide you in all of the things you have to do. When things are good during the day, say thanks. When you need help, encouragement, or insight, ask for it. As you are driving home, reflect on your day and talk with God about it.

As you do this, you will experience the development of God's peace. You will also see yourself walking in confidence personally, professionally, and relationally as you know that there is no part of your life that is left uncovered by prayer and that you are actively talking and listening to God about the things that matter to you most. You are not passively looking for His will through circumstances. You are actively turning to Him and trusting Him through prayer all the time; the peace that only God can give confirms that you are walking in His will for your life.

What does your level of worry say about your relationship with God?

What is the difference between *worry* and *concern?*

IN AMERICAN CULTURE, WE TYPICALLY THINK OF OUR LIVES AS A DISCONNECTED SERIES OF EVENTS. We move from job to job, relationship to relationship, and city to city, leaving the old when we get tired of it and beginning something new. Maybe life is not that disconnected; maybe life should be better thought of in terms of seasons.

The writer of Ecclesiastes reminds us that there is a season for everything in life and that seasons come and go. It's the natural ebb and flow of life, though some seasons are more pleasant than others. Each season provides us an opportunity to seek and experience different aspects of the character of God. In a season of pain, you will experience God differently than in a season of plenty.

Journal this week about your current season of life. Write honestly about your feelings during this season. What are you hoping for? What disappoints you? What satisfies you? Conclude with some reflection about the way you are experiencing God in light of your season.

"LIVING GOD'S WILL IS ABOUT LIVING IN
CONSTANT COMMUNION WITH THE HOLY SPIRIT."

Born in Toulouse, France, Jean-Pierre de Caussade became a member of the Society of Jesus in 1708. He seemed to enjoy anonymity, though his contributions to thinking concerning the will of God are great. His most famous work—indeed the only book he published—is *Spiritual Instructions on the Various States of Prayer.*

GOD'S WILL THROUGH HIS SPIRIT

Not much is known about Jean-Pierre de Caussade. Born in 1675 in Toulouse, France, Caussade was ordained a member of the Society of Jesus in 1708. Never one to enjoy fame, the only book he published remained anonymous for a while and was then attributed to a more popular contemporary.

Nevertheless, there is a phrase that has become identified with his name: "the sacrament of the present moment." According to Caussade, the will of God is not about the big questions of life. It is not even about doing the right thing today. It is about a second-by-second relationship.

Living God's will is about living in constant communion with the Holy Spirit. Without the Spirit and without our submission to Him, there is no chance to live the will of God:

"The presence of God which sanctifies our souls is the Holy Trinity which dwells in our hearts when they surrender to the divine will. God's presence coming to us through an act of contemplation brings this secret union. Like everything else belonging to God's order and enjoined by the divine will, it must always take first place as the most perfect means of uniting ourselves to God.

"It is by being united to the will of God that we enjoy and possess him, and it is a delusion to seek this divine possession by any other means."[11]

GOD'S WILL THROUGH HIS SPIRIT

NEVER GONE

One of the most comforting teachings of Jesus is recorded in Matthew 28:20b:

"And remember, I am with you always, to the end of the age."

In that verse, Jesus promised His abiding presence to His followers for all time. But that's not the first time in Scripture we find a promise like this. I also find comfort in Deuteronomy 31:6, a reminder from Moses to the new leader of Israel, Joshua:

"Be strong and courageous; don't be terrified or afraid of them. For it is the Lord your God who goes with you; He will not leave you or forsake you."

We see God's commitment to His children in these passages. Through Moses' instruction to Joshua, we learn that God is intimately involved in our lives and won't depart from us. Through Jesus' teaching to the disciples, we learn that everywhere we go, Jesus is there, too. He is committed to us until the end of time.

The phrase that stands out to me in these passages is, "He will not leave you or forsake you." While we may acknowledge this intellectually, I wonder if we really believe it. I question how much we believe in God's abiding presence because of the way we pray. At the beginning of worship services, we ask for God to meet us there in that room. We pray that God would "be with" this person or that person during their time of difficulty. Why do we ask God for that which He has already promised? In the form of the Holy Spirit, God is continually with us. We can become more and more conscious of His presence by understanding more and more about the relationship we have with the Holy Spirit.

Perhaps knowing that His disciples were going to struggle to believe in His abiding presence with them, Jesus described in John 16 the new relationship they would have with the Holy Spirit. Essentially, Jesus said that He was leaving, but that He would not be gone. Jesus tried to comfort His disciples by reminding them that it was actually for their benefit that He go to the cross and into eternity with God the Father. They were nevertheless grief-stricken at their impending loss.

As the disciples dried tears of grief and fear from their eyes, Jesus introduced them to the Counselor by describing His ongoing activity in their lives. He said that the Counselor—the Holy Spirit—would come and convict the world in regard to sin, righteousness, and judgment. The Spirit would also guide them in all truth. I can only imagine that their confidence grew as Jesus told them that the Spirit would teach them things that they were not yet ready to hear. He went on to say that the Spirit would only say what He was told to say; He would speak only what He had heard. Even though Jesus was leaving, He would not be gone (John 16:5-15).

This conversation between Jesus and His disciples bears more weight in our lives today than we may realize. Just consider the Spirit's act of conviction. To discern God's will in our day-to-day lives, we need the Spirit to convict us in the three areas Jesus described. First, we need to be convicted of our sin. Without the Spirit's prompting, our hearts will fall away from God rather than grow closer to Him.

Second, we need to be taught what righteousness is. The disciples had witnessed the righteous example of Jesus first-hand for three years, but Jesus knew that even with this experience, His current and future disciples would need to be continually challenged to live rightly. Lastly, the Spirit reminds us of the coming judgment of this world. He tells us that difficult times are not the end of the story and that we should remember the source of our prosperity in the good times.

On the day of Pentecost, all of the believers were together in one place. In my mind, I see them worshiping, praying, sharing stories of Jesus, and enjoying each other's company. While they were there together, the Spirit of God filled the whole house. Tongues of fire came to rest on each of them, and they were filled with the Holy Spirit. Pentecost changed everything (Acts 2:1-13).

The Spirit of God, who once led the nation of Israel with a flaming pillar, was now filling each Christ-follower. He even confirmed this by using the same physical representation He used in the Old Testament—fire. Jesus delivered on His promise; the Counselor had arrived. God's people would never be the same because the Holy Spirit was now active in each of them. People who once visited the temple to worship God had become God's temple (1 Corinthians 3:16). His Spirit took up residence in them!

The Holy Spirit remains a mysterious part of Christianity—both inside and outside the church. For a discussion starter about the Holy Spirit, take a look at the recent documentary *Jesus Camp.*

If you are a believer in Jesus Christ, the Holy Spirit lives in you as well. He is working 24/7 to do all of the things in you that Jesus promised He would do for the disciples. He is working to make you more like Jesus. He is working to show you where God wants you to go. He is working to show you His will so that in every circumstance and in every decision you can know that He is leading you.

What ways have you "heard" the Holy Spirit speak to you?

Is God's abiding presence comforting or disturbing to you? Why?

Listen to "Into the Mystery" by Jason Gray on your playlist.

How do you feel about the mystery of God? Do you embrace it or wish that you had everything figured out?

GUIDE

The Spirit is our teacher and our guide as we read Scripture. Through the power of the Holy Spirit, we are able to understand and apply God's timeless Word. As the Spirit searches our hearts and our minds, nothing goes untouched in this renewal process. In the process, our hearts are transformed and our minds are renewed (Romans 12:1-2). We begin to live our lives based on God's pattern rather than the patterns of the world around us.

Think about it this way: When you read the Bible, you are reading the words that the Spirit inspired. That very same Spirit is now guiding you to discover truth and be transformed into the likeness of Christ. This is a powerful reality: "The Spirit who inspired their writing is perfectly well capable of taking some part of them and writing it on their hearts so that it becomes an inescapable pointer to a particular course of action."[12] Through our study, we learn both with our eyes as we read and with our ears as we listen for God's prompting.

As God transforms our minds, we are empowered to make wise decisions. You don't have to check your brain at the door when it comes to discovering God's will. John Ortberg writes concerning the Spirit's guidance in our lives: "God does not intend that guidance be a shortcut for us to escape making decisions and taking risks."[13] If God is renewing you, and you are seeking Him, He will give you wisdom through the ministry of the Holy Spirit. God generously gives wisdom to those who seek Him by faith (James 1:5-6). God's provision of wisdom allows us to make decisions that we can trust and live out with confidence.

THE GREY AREAS

The Spirit also helps us develop convictions in areas that are not directly referenced in Scripture. These areas are not black-and-white; they are grey. Most of the grey areas in Scripture concern the use of Christian freedom. In the early church, many of these issues centered on what people should eat or not eat or on the religious practices that should carry on from Judaism to Christianity. These were issues of conscience according to the apostle Paul. If your conscience was clear on an issue or a practice, you could practice it freely unless it caused someone else to sin. If your conscience was not clear on an issue or a practice, you should stay clear of it (Romans 14). Somehow, the Spirit of God turns issues of conscience into issues of conviction so that we clearly know the will of God for us in these areas.

God frequently uses the grey areas to remind me in the strangest ways that His Spirit is alive in my life. Not long ago, I was driving home after a long Sunday at church. At a traffic signal, the little, yellow gas light came on in my car. I immediately became excited at the prospect of having to stop for gas: *This is perfect. It's 9:30 at night, I'm going to a gas station, and I haven't eaten in a couple hours—time for a snack.*

My usual snack after all day at church is a Diet Dr. Pepper, a bag of Fritos, and just a little bit of ice cream. After all, if you're going to have chips, you've got to have ice cream. And if you're going to have ice cream, you've got to have chips. So I got the gas and went into the convenience store. I grabbed my drink, chips, and a pint of mint chocolate chip ice cream. As I was standing in line, I noticed that apparently all sorts of people had had a really long day. One of them had a six-pack of beer and was ordering his favorite cigarettes. Another was waiting with some wine coolers. Others held pouches of chewing tobacco. Then there I was with my Diet Dr. Pepper, chips, and ice cream. In my mind, I actually began to think: *Look at all these people with their addictions*. At that moment, I felt the Spirit of God say, "What exactly do you think you're holding, Mike?"

What specific little areas of your life do you think God is concerned about?

Why do they matter to Him so much?

I wish I had the guts at the time to put the ice cream, soda, and chips back, but I didn't. In fact, I chose the longest route home so I could eat and drink it all without my wife finding out. Then, I actually cleaned my car out, because I didn't want anyone to know about my sin. The fact is, I'm just as addicted to soda as I would be to beer if I drank it, and with my family history, ice cream is just as dangerous as a cigarette. That's not to mention the 40 grams of artery-clogging, heart-attack inducing fat in the chips bag.

That night, God reminded me that every area of my life matters to Him. Nowhere in Scripture is ice cream, Diet Dr. Pepper, or Fritos outlawed. Without question, these are grey areas. Yet, the Spirit reminded me that what I eat and what I drink matters. Every part of my life matters to God, and His Spirit has access to it all. God's Spirit is still working on me in this area and many more.

I am committed to working with Him to see my mind and my life transformed so that I can live His will in every area of life. I am committed to this because I know that God's will is better than mine. As I change the patterns of my life, I know I will be able to see more clearly everything God has for me on a daily basis.

THE LITTLE THINGS

But let me clarify—there is not a time when you grow so much in your walk with Christ that you have no need for the Spirit's conviction. In fact, just the opposite happens. Logically, the longer I know Christ, the less I will sin. While it is true that we should sin less as we mature in Christ, it is also true that the sin left in us becomes all the more apparent. As we move toward spiritual maturity, God will continue to bring all sorts of conviction into our lives because He wants our minds to match His mind; He wants no sin to compete with Him.

The book of Song of Solomon reminds us that we should catch the little foxes that ruin our vineyards (Song of Solomon 2:15). While that proverb in its context actually refers to intimacy in marriage, it nevertheless reminds us to look out for the "little sins" that can ruin our lives. Even what we might consider a "little sin" matters to God. It is His will that the Spirit bring all sin to light so that we can take the appropriate steps of obedience.

This passage reminds me of one of my dad's obsessions when I was growing up. In our backyard, we had a small orchard of peach trees. These trees were one of dad's prized possessions because the fruit they produced was amazing. We loved these peaches—and so did the squirrels. Those fruit-stealing vermin became my dad's obsession for the two weeks a year that the peaches were ripe on the tree. Being a kind and gentle man, he trapped the squirrels instead of shooting or poisoning them. Day after day he would trap the thieves, drive them to a wooded area near our house, and release them.

He did this year after year until one day he became convinced that he recognized one of the squirrels. He honestly thought that this squirrel had made the 10-mile trip back to our yard to eat a peach! To prove his hypothesis, he began spray-painting the tails of the squirrels that he trapped and released so that he could know if they were returning.

I can only imagine how the story of these squirrels played out over time. I'm sure that somewhere near Shreveport, Louisiana, there is a

Listen to "Am I Listening?" before your group gets together to discuss this session. (Your group leader will send it to you via e-mail.)

How do you as an individual hear from the Holy Spirit?

house with one of my dad's squirrels mounted on the wall of a proud hunter's home who loves to tell the story: "Well, one day I was just sitting out in the woods hunting when I saw this squirrel run by with a hot pink tail. Then, right behind him was one with a fluorescent green tail. I had to shoot them to protect the rest of our squirrels from these mutants!"

We must bring the same passion—even obsession—to our spiritual lives. We must be so committed to living God's will in every moment that we are willing to go to great lengths to find, mark, and release the sin in our lives, no matter how trivial it might seem.

What are some grey areas in which you would like to have direction from the Lord?

What practical steps can you take to get rid of "the little foxes" in your life?

GOD'S WILL AS THE SPIRIT PROMPTS

To engage in this rooting out of sin, we must be willing to listen to the prompting of the Holy Spirit. If we are listening, we will hear God calling us to action. Sometimes this is an audible voice, but it might simply be a feeling or a sense of direction. In my experience, most of these moments come as the Spirit works to help me apply Scripture to my life. Even after I close the Bible, He is working to see the truth of Scripture fleshed out in my life. He is continually reminding me of ways that I can obey God in tangible, real-life ways. Amazingly, the voice of God usually seems to call us out of our comfort zones. When the Spirit is working like this, you will find yourself thinking, "I have no idea why I am supposed to do this, but I am certain that God wants me to do it."

There are a couple of things you should do when you think the Spirit is prompting you to take action. First, foster an attitude of obedience. You can make the decision in advance to be obedient. Before you even know the question, you can resolve that your answer will be yes. Armed with that resolve, you need to test to ensure that your feeling is actually God prompting you to action and not just the pizza you ate the night before.

Scripture is the litmus test. If what you sense you are being prompted to do is in opposition to the principles of God's Word, then don't take action. If you don't know enough of the Bible to make this decision, do two things. First, start reading and studying your Bible every day so that you will be able to test and approve what the will of God is for your life. Second, talk to your pastor or a trusted friend who can help you sense if this prompting is from God or not.

GOD'S WILL FOR OUR ATTITUDE

The Spirit works in our hearts and minds to remind us that we belong to Christ. He is working in our lives so that our sinful nature is transformed into godly character. The Spirit teaches us and enables us to live a changed life. He is working on us to produce His fruit in our lives.

This provides a pretty easy test to see if you are living God's will when it comes to your attitude and lifestyle. Are you letting the Spirit of God transform you and match your character to God's character? Paul was pretty clear about the character we are to develop. He went so far as to give us a list that describes a Spirit-controlled life: love, joy, peace, patience, kindness, goodness, gentleness, faithfulness, and self-control (Galatians 5:22-23).

He also gave us a list of the acts of the sinful nature: "sexual immorality, moral impurity, promiscuity, idolatry, sorcery, hatreds, strife, jealousy, outbursts of anger, selfish ambitions, dissensions, factions, envy, drunkenness, carousing, and anything similar . . ." (Galatians 5:19-21). Most of us have a blend of the two lists in our lives. Our challenge is to work with the Spirit of God to see His fruit manifested in our lives rather than the acts of the sinful nature that are opposed to the will of God.

GOD'S WILL FOR OUR MINISTRY

The Bible teaches that when we accept Christ, we are given spiritual gifts. Consider God's investment in us: He has gifted everyone who knows Christ. While we are all gifted, we have different gifts according to the grace given us (Romans 12:6). You can read about this truth in 1 Corinthians 12:4-6:

"According to the grace given to us, we have different gifts. . ." (Romans 12:6).

"Now there are different gifts, but the same Spirit. There are different ministries, but the same Lord. And there are different activities, but the same God is active in everyone and everything."

These gifts from the Holy Spirit are for the benefit of the body of Christ. Therefore, we must look to apply our gifts rather than just discover them. It's not about enjoying your giftedness; it's about taking action as God has gifted us. It is God's will that every Christ-follower serve as a part of the body of Christ so that everyone grows to maturity in Christ.

SUBMITTING TO THE SPIRIT'S ACTIVITY

For us to discover the will of God through His Spirit, we must be disciplined enough to submit our lives to the Spirit's activity there. The apostle Paul teaches that we do this by staying in step with the Spirit (Galatians 5:25). It is through staying in step with the Spirit that Paul's prayer in Colossians 1:9 will be fulfilled:

"For this reason also, since the day we heard this, we haven't stopped praying for you. We are asking that you may be filled with the knowledge of His will in all wisdom and spiritual understanding . . . "

According to this passage from Colossians, how does God fill believers today with "wisdom and spiritual understanding"? He fills us with His Spirit. To discover God's will, make it your goal to submit to the Spirit's activity in your life. By doing so, God will fill you with spiritual wisdom and an understanding of His will for your life.

What are some practical ways you can continually listen for the voice of the Holy Spirit?

Do you think the Spirit prompts different people in different ways? Why or why not?

IN GALATIANS 5:25, WE ARE ENCOURAGED THAT "SINCE WE LIVE BY THE SPIRIT, LET US KEEP IN STEP WITH THE SPIRIT" (NIV). It is interesting to think that the Spirit, too, is walking through our lives just as we are. If He, too, is walking, we must ask whether or not we are walking in the same direction, at the same pace, and toward the same destination that He is.

We live in an achievement-based culture. We are urged to set goals and then strive hard after them. Even inside Christian circles, we often use our goals to set our pace and direction and then ask the Holy Spirit to "be with us" after the fact. Instead of having this mentality, Paul argued that we should be looking to the Spirit to set the pace of our walk through life and then match our gait to His.

What sets your pace through life? Are you pushed along by career demands? Are you so motivated by your goals that you are outrunning the Spirit of God? Sit this week with a blank piece of paper and describe your motivations in life. How do those change the way you work, play, and relate to others? Then consider what pace and direction the Spirit is walking. Spend some time listening to Him before you answer.

Notes

Notes

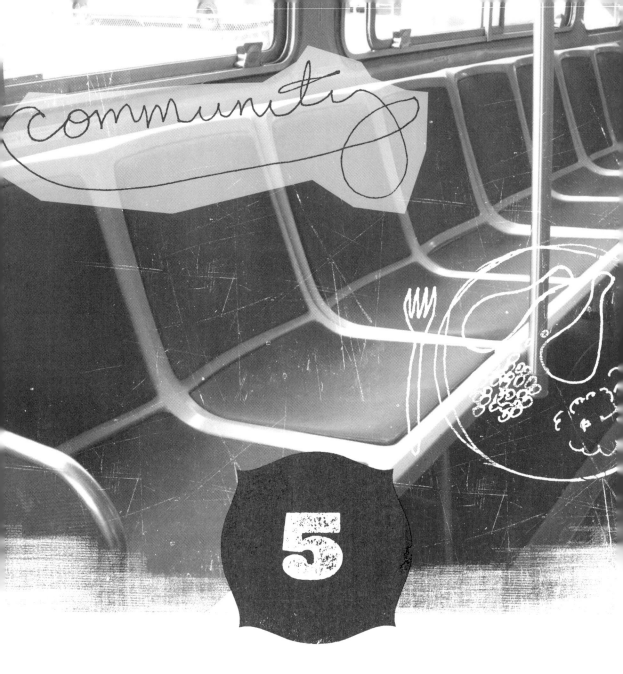

community

5

"IF GOD WANTS US TO BE LIKE JESUS,
RELATIONSHIPS ARE ESSENTIAL TO OUR LIVES."

Martin Luther is best known for his role in the Protestant Reformation. He was born to a peasant family in 1483 and spent his first years with an unending anxiety about his own salvation. Despite entering into the priesthood, his doubt was not relieved until his study led him to Paul's letter to the Romans. This same exercise eventually prompted him to take action and call for church reform. Luther died in 1546.

GOD'S WILL THROUGH COMMUNITY

Life together. That is God's plan.

We are relational creatures by God's design, and yet in our modern culture, we continue to commit the sin of isolation. We withhold ourselves from one another, and in doing so we sin and lead others to do the same.

Likewise, I search for God's will for *my* life. But what if *all* of us were searching for God's will for *your* life? What if the answer does not come to you alone, but together? And what if you can never really see the depth of God's will for you unless you are willing to live in community with others?

Surely there was never a man who knew more loneliness than Martin Luther. In a stand against corruption, Luther started the Reformation on October 31, 1517, when he nailed a list of 95 objections on a castle door. Despite trials, debates, and even excommunication, Luther pressed onward for the purity of the gospel. Perhaps those experiences taught him the value of community:

> "I believe that there is on earth, wide as the world is, not more than one holy general Christian Church, which is nothing else than the community or assembly of the saints. . . . I believe that in this community, or Christendom, all things are common, and each one shares the goods of the others, and none calls anything his own. Therefore all the prayers and good works of the entire community help me and every believer, and support and strengthen us at every time in life and death."[14]

GOD'S WILL THROUGH COMMUNITY

AN ENVIRONMENT FOR DISCOVERY

Relationships are one of the greatest avenues that God has given us for discovering and applying God's will to our lives. Relationships—particularly those with other Christ-followers—cultivate an environment in which you can discover God's will for your life. By developing relationships with others who are committed to their faith in Christ, you will be encouraged to do the same. If it is true that "bad company corrupts good morals" (1 Corinthians 15:34), then the reverse is also true—godly company inspires good morals. Scripture teaches that we can push one another toward Christ in the context of relationships:

"And let us consider how we may spur one another on toward good deeds" (Hebrews 10:24, NIV).

I love the image of spurring one another toward love and good deeds. It gives us a picture of relational rodeo. Spurring one another portrays an active relationship that is potentially risky and at times maybe a little bumpy. God-centered relationships have all of these elements at their core. These relationships are the result of active, intentional friendship-building. They are risky as we learn to trust one another and do life together, and they may be a little bumpy as we work through relational conflict and go through challenging times together. But engaging in God-centered relationships will provide the environment in which you can discover God's will for your life.

Relationships also provide the context for you to live out the will of God in your life. It's impossible to live the will of God outside of relationships. Jesus summed it up when He said we are to love God with our heart, soul, and mind and love our neighbor as ourselves (Matthew 22:36-40). It's interesting to me that Jesus chose the conjunction *and* instead of the conjunction *or*. That means to love God you must love people, and to love people you must love God. All of the Law and the Prophets hang on this truth. Hear it one more time: If we say that we love God, then it is God's will that we express that same love to the people around us—even our enemies.

Why is love central to our relationships? Jesus said:

"By this all people will know that you are My disciples, if you have love for one another" (John 13:35).

Jesus could have chosen any mark He wanted to prove the authenticity of His followers. He could have chosen evangelistic zeal. He could have chosen passionate worship. He could have chosen serving in ministry. But He chose love for one another—biblical community—because loving relationships are the ultimate expression of Christ's activity in our lives. It takes a relationship with God to build truly loving relationships with others. C. S. Lewis wrote:

> "Friendship is—in a sense not at all derogatory to it—the least natural of all loves; the least instinctive, organic, biological, gregarious, and necessary. It has least commerce with our nerves; there is nothing throaty about it; nothing that quickens the pulse or turns you red or pale. It is essentially between individuals . . . without Eros none of us would have been begotten and without Affection none of us would have been reared; but we can live and breed without Friendship."[15]

Do your relationships move you closer or further away from Jesus?

What role do you play in that progress?

Listen to "Does God speak through His people?" before your group gets together to discuss this session. (Your group leader will send it to you via e-mail.)

What relationships in your life help you hear the voice of God?

THE SUPER-SPIRITUAL LONERS

Not everyone agrees that relationships with others are essential to knowing God, obeying God, and consistently discovering the will of God. Some would argue that the truly mature believers don't need others; they have only God, and that is enough. Dr. Henry Cloud and Dr. John Townsend take this issue head on in their book *12 "Christian" Beliefs That Can Drive You Crazy*:

> "The distorted teaching—'If I have God, I don't need people'—says that going to people for our spiritual or emotional needs is wrong. To those who ask for help from other people, teachers of this doctrine say: you lack faith; you have a limited, or small view of God; you are trusting in humans instead of the Savior; you are dabbling in secular humanism; you are in sin; you are proud."[16]

This mind-set sounds super-spiritual to me. The problem with most things that sound overly spiritual is that they are usually wrong. This assumption is no exception. In God's design, we need people. Remember, a relational God designed the world we live in. God Himself lives in relationship with the Son, the Spirit, and the church. If God wants us to be like Jesus, relationships are essential to our lives. Not only does God's nature demand relational connectedness, but Scripture commands it as well.

The Bible is clear: We need one another in the body of Christ. There are more than 50 "one another" commands that outline who we are to be in each other's lives. Eleven of these commands are central to discovering God's will through relationships:

"I give you a new commandment: love one another" (John 13:34-35).

"Show family affection to one another with brotherly love" (Romans 12:10).

"I myself am convinced about you that you also are . . . able to instruct one another" (Romans 15:14).

". . . with patience, accepting one another in love" (Ephesians 4:2).

". . . speaking to one another with psalms, hymns, and spiritual songs" (Ephesians 5:19).

"... submitting to one another in the fear of Christ" (Ephesians 5:21).

"Therefore encourage one another" (1 Thessalonians 4:18).

"Therefore encourage one another and build each other up" (1 Thessalonians 5:11).

"But encourage each other daily" (Hebrews 3:13).

"Spur one another on toward love and good deeds" (Hebrews 10:24, NIV).

"Therefore, confess your sins to one another and pray for one another" (James 5:16).

Along with these "one another" commands, we are commanded to love one another 14 times in the New Testament alone.

By no means is this easy, but Jesus never promised that it would be. In fact, knowing and loving God can actually make our relationships more difficult. After all, we are commanded to forgive those who sin against us. Is that easy? We are commanded to meet one another's physical and spiritual needs. Is that easy? We are commanded to confess our sins to each other. Is that easy? We are commanded to speak the truth in love to each other. Is that easy? Not one of these things are easy to do. None of them are natural for us. That is why they must all be done in an environment of love and grace. Loving relationships are essential to obey the Word of God. It is God's will that you are in loving relationships; otherwise it is impossible to fully obey His Word.

How authentic are you in the relationships you have in your life?

Is it a sin to be alone? Why or why not?

Plan a viewing party of the film *About a Boy*. The movie is an interesting commentary about the need for developing relationships and walking through life together.

COMMITTED RELATIONSHIPS

One of my favorite relationships in Scripture is found in 1 Samuel 18 between David, the future king of Israel, and Jonathan, the son of the reigning king of Israel. You would think that this relationship would be filled with tension and distrust. Instead, their friendship remains an example of the type of relationship that we should all strive to have with at least one other Christ-follower.

There was a purity of commitment and selflessness in the context of the friendship between David and Jonathan. The Bible teaches that Jonathan made a covenant with David because he loved him as himself. He went on to share his most precious possessions with David: his sword, bow, and belt. He even shared the shirt off his back to show how committed he was to his friend.

Committed relationships were also the hallmark of the early church. If I could travel to any time in history, I would choose the first century so that I could be a part of their fellowship. I would love to have experienced the birth of the church as the Holy Spirit came upon believers. I would relish being a member of this fledgling community that committed itself to the apostles' teaching, the breaking of bread, and prayer. I would have treasured being in a community who loved each other so deeply that they even met each other's physical needs. I would give anything to be a part of a group whose reputation and influence was such that people were added to the kingdom daily (Acts 2:41-47).

What set this church apart? They understood that following God meant engaging in loving relationships with the people around them. They were committed to every aspect of each other's lives, and their commitment to each other expressed itself in very practical ways: "'For there was not a needy person among them . . .' (Acts 4:34). Why was that? To hear of a need was to search one's heart to see if one could meet the need."[17] They quickly learned that loving relationships required commitment expressed in action.

Developing this level of commitment will require us to follow the example of David, Jonathan, and the early church and open up our lives to one another. But if I asked you how many true friends you have, my guess is that you would have less than a handful. You may have dozens of acquaintances, but very few deep relationships. The key to developing deep relationships is commitment, and the trigger for commitment is living open lives before each other.

In Germany during World War II, Deitrich Bonhoeffer wrote about the value of living in community.

His classic work, *Life Together,* remains one of the standards on this subject. Take a look.

Don't get me wrong—this will be a stretch. I am in a relationship right now with my friend Todd that is one of my favorite relationships in the world. God has knit both our hearts and our families together, and it excites me. But the other day, I had a "boundary testing" experience with him. We were in my car when Todd reached over to the console and grabbed my ChapStick®. He popped the top and twisted it up four times until there was about a half inch of ChapStick sticking out. He puckered up and casually applied *my* ChapStick to *his* mouth. As I saw all of this out of my peripheral vision, I said, "Dude, what are you doing?" Without a word, he spun it back, put the top back on, and threw it back into its resting place.

I told him in no uncertain terms, "You may as well keep it. I'm never using it again." A couple days later, Todd walked into my office with a brand new stick of ChapStick that said, "To Mike, from Todd." It's still sitting on my desk.

The ChapStick on my desk reminds me that I need to stretch myself in my relationships. I'm not telling you to share ChapStick. Frankly, I think that's just gross. Instead, I'm encouraging you to step out of your comfort zone. Share. Give. Receive—and do so in uncomfortable ways so that you can develop growing, committed relationships with other Christ-followers.

Committed relationships are essential to discovering God's will because they provide an environment of love and grace. We all need "safe" relationships in which we can ask tough questions about life while knowing that nothing we do or say will cause our friends to think any less of us. We all need grace-filled relationships so that when our life doesn't match up with God's intent, our friends can gently restore us to the life God intends. If you know you are engaged in relationships that express their commitment in love and grace, you will have the confidence to chase God's will for your life because you will know that no matter what happens, you are not standing alone.

What is the most difficult part of having relationships that stretch you?

INTENTIONAL RELATIONSHIPS

Taking our committed relationships to the next level requires intentionality. Intentional relationships are "on purpose" friendships. They are not incidental or indifferent; they are committed relationships that exist to help you become more like Jesus. It is essential that we have people in our lives who hold us to God's standard of living.

Every friendship is not intentional, at least by this definition, and that's OK. It's OK to have friends from work who you like to have lunch with. It's OK to be in a fantasy football league with old friends from college. It's OK if you have an exercise partner at the gym. It's not OK, though, if all of your relationships are at this level. We all need people who will purposefully push us to be more like Jesus.

Over the years, Christians have incorrectly attempted to over-program and over-simplify these relationships. Intentional relationships are multifaceted—a blend of service, encouragement, accountability, confession, and much more. The list goes on and on because God can use every part of our relationships to make us more like Christ if we are intentional in our dealings with one another.

INTENTIONALITY VS. ACCOUNTABILITY

One of the most misunderstood ingredients of an intentional relationship is accountability. If your church experience has been like mine, then it probably feels like accountability relationships have been forced down your throat. Accountability was sold to us as the ultimate expression of Christian vulnerability and the secret to overcoming the peskiest sins in our lives. The only problem is that the "accountability" in most churches is neither an intimate experience nor a panacea for our sin problem.

Instead, it is a time when we come together to answer some prescribed questions that are supposed to measure our spirituality. If we failed that week, we have our spiritual hand slapped. If we didn't fail in these areas, we are encouraged to do the same next week even if we failed in other areas of life that were not covered in the all too generic questions we were asked.

We all need accountability, but few of us need the type of relationship that I have just described. We need a mind-set shift when it comes to accountability, because real accountability is less about talking through rote questions and more about intentionality. I love the way Sheryl Fleisher defines it: "Accountability is taking people kicking and screaming where they really want to be."[18] You see, accountability is about helping people keep their commitments to God, and that is an ever-changing, organic process.

I don't know about you, but the issues that God is working on in me this year are different than the issues He was working on last year and are vastly different than the issues from 10 years ago. That is why intentional relationships are so much better than accountability relationships when it comes to discovering and applying God's will to our lives. Because the questions of life change, we should not just seek to answer the same old list of questions correctly. Rather, we should learn how we can ask the right questions at the right time so that our intentional relationships result in life-change rather than just right answers.

> How is this perspective of accountability different than others you have heard?

Recently, my youngest daughter started preschool. When my wife went to pick her up at the end of the first day of school, the teachers sheepishly greeted her and said that there were a couple of issues with Rebekah that day. Apparently, Bekah took off her clothes repeatedly throughout the day. To the teacher's dismay, my wife was not shocked. Changing clothes is a hobby for Bekah. She will change five to six times a day if we let her. Evidently, she felt comfortable at school, so it was time to shed those clothes. While we thought this was somewhat humorous, we knew that we needed to talk to her.

So when I got home from work, I sat down with her and talked through the issue. She was pretty embarrassed by the conversation, so I tried to be as gentle as possible. I asked her one simple question: "Do you think that Daddy takes off his pants when he goes to work?" Thankfully, she did not. So I told her to follow my example and keep her clothes on outside of the house. She said, "OK, Daddy," and I assumed we were done. Three days later, however, I came home from work, and she asked me, "Did you take your pants off at work, Daddy?"

"And they devoted themselves to the apostles' teaching, to fellowship, to the breaking of bread, and to prayers" (Acts 2:42).

I told her no. Every night, she asks me the same question and updates me on her ability to remain clothed all day. Now, you could argue that our conversations are a form of accountability.

But what if my question to Bekah never changes? What if the only thing I ever ask her about her life and the challenges she faces is whether or not she keeps her clothes on? Will that one question cover the multitude of issues that she will face as she grows to become the woman God intends for her to be? It may be the exact question to ask in her teenage years, but it's not the only question that I will ask her to intentionally help her live God's will for her life. The questions of life will change, but my commitment to intentionally develop her faith will not.

> Given this definition, which of your current relationships are truly "accountability" relationships?

Listen to "I'm Not the Only One Asking" by Mindy Smith on your playlist.

How many of us are asking the same questions? What if we were asking them on behalf of each other?

THE DISCIPLINE OF CONNECTION

For people to play a key role in your discovery of God's will, you will need to practice the discipline of connection to other believers. Some people call this fellowship, but in today's church culture, we have minimized fellowship by defining it as any event where food is served. The all too common "food, fun, and fellowship" alliteration has entered the church's vocabulary, and in doing so, has led the church to be committed to *fellowship* rather than *the fellowship* of believers.

Read Acts 2:42 and you will see a body of believers who is committed to *the fellowship*—to intimate, caring relationships with each other rather than just hanging out together. They expressed this discipline by worshiping together in the temple daily and meeting in each other's homes. This was not just fellowship; it was connection between Christ-followers.

Connection does not happen by accident for most of us. It takes discipline. Discipline is required to stay connected to the vital relationship environments that God uses to communicate His will through other believers. The early church's pattern of worship in the temple and meeting from house to house provides a solid pattern for us if we are to live a connected life.

INVOLVED IN THE CHURCH

Every Christ-follower needs a real-time connection with a church—the local body of believers. None of us can survive, let alone thrive, in our faith without this. We need a real-time connection that involves face-to-face, corporate worship experiences. Don't be tempted to let virtual community become an incomplete substitution for the relationships that are established through the church. Also, don't run from Christian event to Christian event and consider that *church*. Conferences and concerts are great, but they are not church. We all need a local body of believers with whom we grow, connect, and worship.

Through this local church experience, God will reveal His will to us. As we worship and pray corporately, we will hear God's voice. He will speak to us as we hear His Word taught through our pastor. He will reveal His character to us as we use our gifts. All of this will result in the maturation of our faith and our understanding of God's will for our lives.

ACTIVE IN A GROUP

Along with large group worship opportunities, we all need small group experiences as a means to discover and apply God's will for our lives. Small groups provide the environment for growth because a consistent group of people can learn to live life intimately together over time. Small groups provide an opportunity for us to study and serve together so we discover God's will both through the truth of His Word and the experiences of our lives as we live out His Word. Groups also provide people with whom you can live out the "one another" commands we find in the Bible.

Small groups are indispensable in your development as a Christ-follower because they force you to personalize your faith. You can hide from difficult questions and faith struggles when you are in a corporate worship service, but it is much harder to remain anonymous when you are in a group of 8 to 12 people whose chief purpose is growth toward maturity.

When the group studies, you are asked to apply the principles to your life. When the group prays, you are encouraged to share your needs and concerns through requests. When the group serves, you tag along even if you aren't exactly interested in serving. When group members struggle or have needs, you are given the opportunity to meet their needs like only you can. Everything is personalized

"Not staying away from our meetings, as some habitually do, but encouraging each other, and all the more as you see the day drawing near" (Hebrews 10:25).

through a small group experience. This leads you to discover God's will for your life because you are doing things together that you might never do without the group.

> What keeps you from viewing your church as a place to find God's will for your life?

> What are some ways you could help others in your church find God's will for their lives?

SEEKING GODLY ADVICE

Not only will living a connected life give you a place in which you will discover and apply God's will to your life, it will also give you people to whom you can turn for godly wisdom. This is how you take your community from good to great. Turn to each other and ask for help and advice when you are facing difficult circumstances or substantial life decisions. You don't have to live life alone, and you don't have to make every decision yourself.

Throughout the Book of Proverbs, we learn the benefit of trusting others to discover God's activity and direction for our lives:

"Without guidance, people fall, but with many counselors there is deliverance" (Proverbs 11:14).

"A fool's way is right in his own eyes, but whoever listens to counsel is wise" (Proverbs 12:15).

"Wisdom is gained by those who take advice" (Proverbs 13:10).

"Plans fail for lack of counsel, but with many advisers they succeed" (Proverbs 15:22).

"Listen to counsel and receive instruction so that you may be wise in later life" (Proverbs 19:20).

"Finalize plans through counsel . . ." (Proverbs 20:18).

"The sweetness of a friend is better than self-counsel"
  (Proverbs 27:9).

The common words in many of these verses are counsel, advice, or
advisors. Before you run out and look for advice from everyone under
the sun, consider the qualities of those advising you. The first quality
you want is **spiritual maturity**. Make sure that the people you go to
will point you to God and not just common sense. Next, look for those
who **wisely apply the truth** of God to their own lives. Do you respect
who they are and who they are becoming? If not, why go to them?
The last quality to look for is **commitment**. Don't look for someone
who just wants to fix your problem; look for someone committed and
able to walk with you through the decision-making process.

It's vital to find these qualities in the people we turn to for godly
advice because we are trusting them with our lives, talking through
questions of what we should say, do, think, or feel. They advise us with
godly insight. You then take action based on their recommendations
in the context of what God has been teaching you through His
Word and by His Spirit. In a sense, you've given them at least shared
ownership of your future. If you find the right person to engage in this
type of mentoring or discipleship relationship, it can be one of the
most fruitful relationships that you will ever experience.

What are some other qualities you want in advisors?

Should you seek advice from people older than you?
Why or why not?

JESUS IS INCREDIBLY CONCERNED ABOUT HOW WE TREAT ONE ANOTHER.

In his first letter, John goes so far as to say that those who do not love other people cannot claim they love God (1 John 4:7-8). The love of God is so rich and encompassing that it fills our cup and overflows into our community of relationships.

However, much of our culture has been structured to prize individualism. We want our own achievements. We want our own possessions. We want our own fame. And we want God's will for our own lives.

This week, choose two of the "one another" commands listed in this chapter. Memorize those verses along with specific ways to apply them in specific relationships in your life. Seek to walk in a counter cultural way and be community-minded rather than individual-minded.

Notes

6

"ONLY THOSE WHO HAVE WRESTLED WITH A SILENT GOD ARE READY TO HEAR HIM SPEAK AGAIN."

Born in Fantiveros, Sastile, in Spain, John of the Cross (1542-1591) spent his life trying to reform the church he loved. His work led him to be arrested and imprisoned. He wrote notably about suffering and commitment examining the place of sorrow and darkness in the Christian life.

THE SILENCE OF GOD

At one time or another, all of us seeking the will of God come to a place in our journey that seems impassable. Some have called this season the *desert*. Others have referred to it as the *wilderness*. John of the Cross called it something else:

"At a certain point in the spiritual journey, God will draw a person from the beginning stage to a more advanced stage. At this stage the person will begin to engage in religious exercises and grow deeper in the spiritual life.

"Such souls will likely experience what is called 'the dark night of the soul.' The 'dark night' is when those persons lose all the pleasure that they once experienced in their devotional life. This happens because God wants to purify them and move them on to greater heights."[19]

John became a monk in 1564. Teresa of Avila saw his great potential and put him in charge of his order because of his self-discipline and leadership ability. His contemporaries nicknamed him "John of the Cross" because of his unwavering commitment and loyalty in the face of suffering.

Surely there were times when John didn't hear God. He didn't feel God. He certainly couldn't see God. Yet John believed that this "dark night" was not God's abandonment or punishment but an essential part of the journey toward maturity.

Only those who have wrestled with a silent God are ready to hear Him speak again.

THE SILENCE OF GOD

POWER OUTAGE

The power went out in my house as I was writing this study. In a split second, the lights went out, the TV went off, the AC stopped running, the Internet router went dead, and the phone stopped working. The house was completely silent except for the screams of my three young children. Experiencing darkness is a scary thing, but the feelings of isolation and alarm quickly subsided as we lit a candle and waited for life to return to normal. Normal for us came an hour and 45 minutes later when our power was restored.

My guess is that we have all experienced a loss of power in our homes. I am also pretty confident that most of us have experienced a seeming power outage in our relationships with God as well. There has been a time in our lives when it seems like things between God and us have gone dark—no more comfort; no more communication; nothing.

Author Ken Gire appropriately calls this a wilderness experience. Experiences like these can make us feel the kind of feelings we might experience in the wilderness: paranoia, doubt, fear, isolation, loneliness, and confusion. Gire experienced his own wilderness when he quit his job to become a writer. As a result of this faith decision, he and his family experienced one of the most painful periods of their lives. Since writing a book doesn't put food on the table, the family quickly burned through their savings. This forced them to make multiple moves, disconnecting them from their spiritual communities. He was confident of his call; however, that didn't make his wilderness experience any less painful. His experience in the wilderness was full of doubt and anxiety, pain and humiliation. The wilderness is a time when we cry out until our lungs ache only to hear a deafening silence in return.

If we think through our lives, many of us can relate to Gire's feelings when it comes to wilderness or desert experiences in life. Maybe you experienced a dry time with God following the death of a loved one because you could not understand why God would take them. Maybe you sought God's will after a break-up in a relationship, and you heard nothing in return. Maybe you are looking for new things in your career and nothing has surfaced, so you wonder what God wants you to do. Maybe you have not been passionately pursuing God lately.

Listen to "What if I can't hear anything?" before your group gets together to discuss this session. (Your group leader will send it to you via e-mail.)

Have you ever felt like God was silent? What did it feel like?

You have allowed your faith to grow lukewarm rather than white-hot, and as a result, you feel distanced and disconnected from God. Maybe you took a great risk for God, and in your eyes, He did not live up to His part of the deal.

Though each of us enters the wilderness in different ways, we can all relate to the common feelings of doubt, discouragement, despair, and disbelief. To survive these feelings, we must understand why we are where we are and what God's will is for us in these seasons of life.

> Describe a time you have spent in the spiritual wilderness. What caused you to be there?

> How do you think God feels when you are in the wilderness?

WHY THE WILDERNESS?

If God's ultimate will for our lives is for us to be like Jesus, don't you think that He is going to do some of the same things in our lives that He did in His Son's while He walked among us? If that is the case, then wilderness experiences should be expected rather than feared. Jesus, by my count, had two such experiences in just three years of public ministry.

Jesus' own wilderness experiences are recorded in Matthew 4:1-11 and Matthew 26:42-46.

It's interesting to note that Jesus, like Adam thousands of years earlier, was tempted with food.

Read the account in Genesis 3:1-7 and note the similarities of the temptations but the differences of response.

His first came just after His baptism. He spent 40 days fasting and wrestling with the devil in the wilderness. It was in this first wilderness experience that Jesus' allegiance was tested. The devil tempted Him to see if He would stay committed to God. Satan encouraged Him to turn a rock into bread. Jesus side-stepped this invitation to break His fast with the confession "Man must not live on bread alone but on every word that comes from the mouth of God" (Matthew 4:4). Score one for Jesus. Even though He had been fasting for more than a month, He knew God's provision for Him was more than adequate.

Having been unsuccessful in tempting Christ to trust His needs to something other than the Father, Satan moved to the temptation of power. He took Jesus to the highest point of the temple and told Him that he would give Him authority over everything visible. Again Jesus refused, knowing that all authority had already been given to Him.

The devil then challenged Jesus to prove God's love for Him. He told Him to throw Himself off the temple. Surely, God would send a legion of angels to save His Son. Jesus' response: "It is also written: Do not test the Lord your God" (Matthew 4:7).

So what can we learn from Jesus' first wilderness experience? The affections of our hearts are tested when we are in the wilderness. When we are tired, lonely, and hungry, who are we going to turn to? Will we trust God's provision or take action on our own? Will we wait for God, or will we attempt a miracle by our own hands? In the wilderness, our motives are clarified, and our dependence on God is essential for survival.

If I told you that in the next 40 days, I could help you fall more in love with Jesus; that you would learn how to depend on Him more; and that you would see your heart begin to transform, I bet you would take me up on my offer. At the surface, it's an easy invitation to accept. But as you look deeper into this invitation, you begin to realize that all of those benefits involve a high level of sacrifice, struggle, and uncertainty concerning the future. This is not an invitation to a retreat center; it's an invitation to the wilderness. So knowing that, would you still accept it?

ABSOLUTE CONFIDENCE

I'm pretty sure Jesus would. He actually *pursued* wilderness experiences like the one I just described. It was during His second wilderness experience that Jesus was desperate to confirm God's will for His own life. Just before His arrest, trial, and crucifixion, Jesus withdrew with three of His trusted friends. His goal was to pray—pray that God would clearly communicate His will to Him. Jesus had to know for sure what the Father wanted.

He was overwhelmed by what lay ahead of Him on the cross, so He entered the garden to seek God and His will. What followed was one of the most passionate prayer experiences ever recorded.

"Going a little farther, He fell facedown and prayed, 'My Father! If it is possible, let this cup pass from Me. Yet not as I will, but as You will'" (Matthew 26:39).

Hear the confidence of Jesus in this prayer: "God, I know that You can do anything. You could take this cup from Me. I only want to do what You want Me to do, so I am looking for Your will on this subject and not just Mine."

After finding His disciples sleeping rather than praying as He told them to do, He prayed this same prayer a second time. Again, He voiced a prayer confident in God and committed to doing His will. Following these passionate prayers, Jesus knew what He had to do, and minutes later, He was arrested.

For Christ, the result of this wilderness experience was absolute confidence that He was living the will of God. It's interesting to me that even Jesus needed this level of assurance. He set the example for us as we look to confidently walk in God's will for our lives. In the midst of what I can only imagine was the most difficult night of His life, He expressed His confidence in God through prayer not just once, but twice. In the midst of incredible physical pain (remember He sweat blood), He turned to God through prayer not just once, but twice. In the midst of friends who did not keep their commitments, Jesus drew closer to His Father not just once, but twice. In the midst of all of this, He was able to pray for God's will rather than His own. Nothing would dissuade Him from confirming God's will in His life.

For Henri Nouwen's discussion of how to live and thrive during the wilderness days, check out *Turn My Mourning into Dancing*.

Consider how this confirmation in the garden of Gethsemane pulled Jesus through what would come next. Do you think Jesus thought of the confirmation He received in the garden when Peter wanted to protect Him by the sword? What about when He was taken before unrighteous judges who were more concerned with personal interests than doing the right thing?

Or maybe did He think of the garden confirmation as He was beaten, mocked, and spat upon by vicious soldiers? Perhaps it came to mind as He was ridiculed by the religious people of the day? Maybe He recalled it as He hung on the cross and saw His friends and family crying? Do you think that Jesus thought of that confirmation as He turned His eyes to heaven and said, "Father, forgive them, because they do not know what they are doing" (Luke 23:34)?

How do wilderness experiences prepare you for the future?

How do you think God feels when you seek Him in the wilderness?

WALKING THROUGH THE WILDERNESS

It's clear that wilderness experiences are a key ingredient in God's plan to shape your life. God sent Moses to the desert for 40 years to prepare him to lead Israel out of captivity. Jacob wrestled with God in the wilderness. Even Jesus spent time in the "desert" as a part of His preparation for ministry. As a result, each of these men knew God more intimately and clearly discovered God's will for their lives. But notice, too, that for each of these men, there was a designated time that they were in the wilderness.

For Jacob, it was a night. For Jesus, it was 40 days. For Moses, it was 40 years. It seems clear that though God might lead you to the wilderness, it is not His intention for you to live there. When God's desired activity is complete in you, He will bring you out of the desert. Unfortunately, there is no way to know how long you will be in a desert experience. This is based on God's timing and our response to His work in our lives. There are a few things that we can do, though, as we walk through the wilderness.

First, consider your focus. Ensure that you are pursuing God and His will. Focus on His activity and action in your life. Don't just look out for your own interests, but look for His direction and His purposes. Look to build your life on faith rather than certainty. You may be experiencing a desert experience today so that God can refresh you tomorrow.

Gary Thomas writes that God leads us to the desert "so that He can irrigate our desert with the cold water of pure faith, so He can break our addiction to the sensual and call us to the truly spiritual, and so that we can say without doubt or need for refreshment, 'O God, You are my God, and I will follow You all of my days.'"[20]

Second, check your motives. James 4:3 reminds us that motives matter to God. If God is the one who holds your future in His hands and He also knows your heart and what drives you, why would He tell you what you should do next if your motives are out of whack?

Third, consider your maturity level. You may be asking for something that you are not spiritually ready for. God's desire is that all things will make you more like Jesus, but He will not put you into a place that you are not ready for. Moses was not ready to lead Israel from Pharaoh's captivity until he spent 40 years in the Midian desert.

"You ask and don't receive because you ask wrongly, so that you may spend it on your desires for pleasure" (James 4:3).

It was only after Moses was prepared that God called him. If you are in the middle of your desert experience, don't give up. God's timing is always right. I have often heard Pastor Lon Solomon say that the burning bush is never early. It's never late. It's always right on time.

Consider also Jacob's wrestling match in the wilderness at the ford of the Jabbok River. Jacob was on his way to meet with his brother, Esau, when he found himself in the fight of his life—or at least the fight that would change his life. Hear how the prophet Hosea tells it:

"Jacob struggled with the Angel and prevailed; he wept and sought His favor. He found him at Bethel, and there He spoke with him. Yahweh is the God of Hosts; Yahweh is His name" (Hosea 12:4-5).

What Hosea doesn't tell us is how this royal rumble affected Jacob. Genesis 32 records that Jacob had a wrestling match with a mysterious person that night by the river. The fight was long and hard with neither figure overpowering the other. As dawn approached, Jacob's opponent revealed the true extent of his power when he touched Jacob's hip so that it was wrenched as they wrestled.

But even this move did not end the match. Jacob refused to release him until the man blessed him—and bless him he did. He blessed him with a new name, Israel, because he had struggled with God and with man and had overcome. Jacob then got up and named the place Peniel because he had seen God face to face and had survived. As he limped away, he was a changed man because of his time in the wilderness.

We need to see our desert experiences as an opportunity to wrestle with God as Jacob did. Our society sees difficult times, troubling circumstances, and desert experiences as a necessary evil. To many, these are nothing more than unfortunate days to just try to get through. One of the ways this is expressed is in a very confusing maxim: What doesn't kill you only makes you stronger. To me, the math doesn't add up on this one. Sometimes it's true, at least in the movies, but most of the time, hard times don't produce strong people. More often, hard times produce doubt, discouragement, and depression.

Listen to "The Silence of God" by Andrew Peterson on your playlist. Then listen some more.

What does the silence sound like? What might prompt God to remain silent?

As Christ-followers, we need to turn this cliché on its head. Instead of just looking for that very elusive strength through difficult circumstances, we need to see every challenge we face as an opportunity to draw near to God; if you draw near to God, He will give you strength and perseverance. He will work to change you to the core even through the most difficult experiences.

Do you think most people draw closer or further away from God during wilderness times? Why?

What is your tendency? Why?

HOLDING ON

It's tough to turn to God when He is the one you are mad at. If you are in a desert experience right now, God may be the last person you want to talk to. You have been diligently searching for His will. You have been praying. You have been listening to His Spirit. You have sought godly counsel. You have looked wisely at your circumstances and still heard nothing from God. Right now, the way you see it, God has let you down.

The reality is that even though you may feel abandoned, God is at work in you. In Philippians 1:6, we learn that we can be . . .

". . . sure of this, that He who started a good work in you will carry it on to completion until the day of Christ Jesus."

Hear this: If you are seeking God by faith that results in obedience that glorifies Him, He has not left you and He is not done with you. If you are in the midst of a desert experience, the last thing you want to hear is that God is at work even if it doesn't seem like it. You don't want to hear this because it somehow minimizes the pain and discouragement that you're feeling. Then, maybe you begin to wonder if it's right to feel the way that you do. Before you know it, you begin to distance yourself from God and from the people around you who continually give you that "spiritual pep talk."

While you don't want to hear it, the truth that God is at work is exactly what you need to remember in the deserts of your life. Though you wrestle, though you doubt, though you worry, God's will for you is to continue to hold onto Him—even violently so—during these desert experiences of life. He wants to work on you, in you, and through you as a result of your time in the desert with Him. If you hold on, you will walk differently just as Jacob did after your own experience in the desert. Ken Gire summed up his wilderness experience and the effect it had on his life like this: "All of which were necessary for me to experience if I was to be the writer I needed to be, wanted to be, prayed to be. . . Seminary prepared me to use my gift. The wilderness prepared me to live my life."[21]

The lessons that we learn in the desert can be summed up in three words: die to self. It's in the desert experiences of our lives that we discover firsthand what it means to put our hopes, dreams, concerns, and fears into God's hands. We learn how we can trust God even when we are unsure of His activity and, as a result, uncertain of our future. We learn how to become men or women of faith as we give every circumstance of life over to Him. We learn how to live life by risky, God-centered devotion because He has become our only source for life and hope. In the desert, we have no other choice—it is God's will for our lives or nothing at all.

LIMPING AWAY

All of this prepares us to live the life that God has marked out for us. Because of the desert experiences, we walk with God differently. Remember, Jacob walked with a limp after he wrestled with God. This was not a pulled muscle or sprain that he could simply walk off—his life was altered because of his time in the desert. Jesus spent 40 days in the desert preparing for His public ministry. Even Satan's failed efforts to tempt Him clarified Jesus' purpose on earth. Then, just three years later, Jesus was in the desert again looking for confirmation of God's will. He prayed the ultimate prayer of faith, "not My will, but Yours, be done" (Luke 22:42).

If you practice the discipline of dying to yourself even in the most challenging circumstances in your life, I am confident that God will do in you what He did for Jacob and Jesus. You will walk differently with God because you are dying to yourself and living for Him. As you do this, He will continue to clarify your purpose and give you the courage to live it out no matter what Satan or others throw at you. Ultimately, He will lead you to a point of utter dependence on Him where you will find yourself praying Jesus' prayer, "Not my will, but Your will be done."

That sort of pursuit is much better than an attempt at finding the answers to "The Big Three" questions of life. Finding God's will is much more about this attitude of relational submission than about God passing out pieces of vital information. God wants to be much more than an answer-spitting slot machine in our lives. He wants to be our Master. He wants to be our Companion. He wants to be our Father.

He wants us to question Him about the key issues of life, but He wants those questions to come inside the context of an ongoing relationship based on mutual love. He wants us to desire *Him* more than we desire *answers*. As we walk in relationship with Him as our Father, we can also trust that each step of the way He will, in His time, steer our path the way it needs to go.

NOISE IS EVERYWHERE. Consider your life: How many things do you have in your life that drown out the silence? With a cell phone, iPod, television, laptop, and car radio there is hardly any room for peace and quiet. We fill our lives with ways to be connected with technology, work, and each other, but also because we fear the silence.

What if you spent an entire afternoon with no technology? What if there was nothing there to distract you? What would you hear? Perhaps nothing, and that is especially disconcerting. When we rid our lives of the noise and find that there is silence—just silence—we are left to contemplate the difficult questions that remain about who we are and who God is.

This week, pick an afternoon to embrace silence. Don't try to get away anymore; confront the fear of silence and embrace what you find there. In God's silence, you may hear more than you expect.

Notes

Notes

END NOTES

SESSION 1

1 Stanley I. Stuber, *Basic Christian Writings* (New York: Association Press, 1957), 15-16.

2 Rich Hurst, *Courage to Connect* (Colorado Springs: Chariot Victor Publishing, 2002), 60.

3 *www.snopes.com/autos/techno/cruise.asp*

SESSION 2

4 Richard J. Foster and James Bryan Smith, *Devotional Classics* (New York: HarperCollins Publishers, 1993), 321.

5 *http://dictionary.reference.com/browse/meditation*

6 Dallas Willard, *The Spirit of the Disciplines* (London: Hodder & Stoughton Religious, 1996), 176.

SESSION 3

7 Stanley I. Stuber, *Basic Christian Writings* (New York: Association Press, 1957), 41-42.

8 Millard J. Erikson, *Christian Theology* (Grand Rapids: Baker Academic, 1998), 413.

9 *www.probe.org/content/view/947/147/#text1*

10 A. W. Tozer, *The Knowledge of the Holy* (New York: HarperSanFrancisco, 1992), 110-111.

SESSION 4

11 Richard J. Foster and James Bryan Smith, *Devotional Classics* (New York: HarperCollins Publishers, 1993), 232.

12 Michael Green, *I Believe in the Holy Spirit* (Grand Rapids: Wm. B. Eerdmans Publishing Company, 2004), 95.

13 John Ortberg, *The Life You've Always Wanted* (Grand Rapids: Zondervan, 2002), 150.

SESSION 5

14 Stanley I. Stuber, *Basic Christian Writings* (New York: Association Press, 1957), 51-52.

15 C. S. Lewis, *The Four Loves* (New York: Harvest Books, 1971), 58.

16 Dr. Henry Cloud and Dr. John Townsend, *12 "Christian" Beliefs That Can Drive You Crazy* (Grand Rapids: Zondervan, 1995), 115.

17 Peter H. Davids, *More Hard Sayings of the New Testament*, (London: Hodder & Stoughton Religious, 1991), 44.

18 Sheryl Fleisher, Willow Creek Small Groups Conference: Intentional Discipleship Breakout Seminar, 2000

SESSION 6

19 Richard J. Foster and James Bryan Smith, *Devotional Classics* (New York: HarperCollins Publishers, 1993), 33.

20 Gary L. Thomas, *Seeking the Face of God* (Irvine: Harvest House Publishers, 1999), 187.

21 Ken Gire, *Windows of the Soul* (Grand Rapids: Zondervan, 1996), 104.

take a sneak peak at another study from Threads

GET UNCOMFORTABLE
SERVE THE POOR. STOP INJUSTICE. CHANGE THE WORLD... IN JESUS' NAME

TABLE OF CONTENTS

SERVE THE POOR. STOP INJUSTICE. CHANGE THE WORLD... IN JESUS' NAME.

LETTING GO OF THE TABLE

When my son Parker was learning how to walk, he would use the coffee table in our living room to pull himself up and then walk around the table for hours at a time. He spent days walking around and around that table, smiling and giggling the whole time. For a time, he was very content not to venture beyond the safety of the table. After about a week, he seemed to be getting a little bored (or dizzy) from the monotony of walking in circles, but he didn't know what to do next.

Then, for no obvious reason, one morning he walked to the corner of the table, but instead of turning to follow the table around the corner, he took an extra step forward and found himself standing on his own, hands in the air. I could tell he was thinking, "Wow! Here I am out here in the middle of the room with no table holding me up!" He began to giggle and then fell right down on his bottom. That was the beginning. From that moment on, he never walked around that table again. He would go to that same corner, pull himself up, turn away from the table, and take a step. Everything had changed.

NEVER GOING BACK

The moment a child takes his or her first steps is special but not strictly because of the steps. If the journey ended at that point, then the whole process would be woefully anti-climactic. Letting go of the table is thrilling because of what it symbolizes; for when a child lets go, they are never going back. Those first, tentative, uncertain steps mean that the proverbial gun has been shot at the beginning of a great race.

This same child who found out several years ago that he could stand on his own two feet is now running around the soccer field like Pelé. He is amazing! He runs with purpose. He no longer has to devote all of his attention to each tentative step. He doesn't have to think, "I now need to put my right foot forward to keep from falling." There's no longer any forethought in the process; his body simply moves. It runs. It's agile. Running is no longer something that Parker tries to do; running is now part of who Parker is.

The baby steps were a good and necessary part of the process of making Parker a runner. The goal however was not tentative steps in the living room but intuitive movement in the world. The goal is to be a runner—to make running second nature in order to open up the world beyond the coffee table.

In the very same way, each of us will have an opportunity through this study to let go of the table. Many of us are living our Christian lives holding on to the programs, events, and comfort of our local church. Many of us have never ventured out from these programs—Sunday service, Wednesday dinner, weekly Bible study, and the annual Christmas gift drive. When no one is around, we wonder, "Is this all there is?" "Is this all that we're supposed to do and be as the people of God?" "Is there something more to this Christian life?" "Did God put us on this earth just to keep the believers happy in their church buildings?" All of these church activities are good and have their place in the process, but they are just that—a part of a much larger process.

ZECHARIAH 7:9–10A
THE LORD OF HOSTS SAYS THIS: "RENDER TRUE JUSTICE. SHOW FAITHFUL LOVE AND COMPASSION TO ONE ANOTHER. DO NOT OPPRESS THE WIDOW OR THE FATHERLESS, THE STRANGER OR THE POOR . . ."

EMBRACING SELF-FORGETFULNESS

In the Christian life, the programs of the local congregation that are centered on meeting the needs of the members are the Christian equivalent of walking around the coffee table. They were never meant to be the sum of the Christian life. A mature believer develops what I call a "healthy sense of self-forgetfulness" rather than an unhealthy preoccupation with self. Jesus demanded that if we would truly follow him, then we must deny ourselves (Luke 9:23). There is an unbelievably huge world out there in need of believers who have denied themselves, let go of the table, and become runners in God's race to increase His eternal kingdom through Jesus Christ.

I'm not talking about more activities, because we certainly don't need that. We are all very busy Christians. But busy believers are not necessarily mature believers. Just because we are going to a lot of activities doesn't mean we are growing in our faith. Just because we're engaged in daily devotion doesn't mean we are becoming a fully devoted follower of Christ. We all must move from internally focused involvement in the church to externally focused engagement with our world in the name of Christ. We must all, at some moment in time, let go of the table.

A MATURE BELIEVER DEVELOPS WHAT I CALL A "HEALTHY SENSE OF SELF-FORGETFULNESS" RATHER THAN AN UNHEALTHY PREOCCUPATION WITH SELF.

BECOMING A PART OF THE SOLUTION

Through this study, we will each have an opportunity to do just that—let go—and venture out into the world on our own two feet into the realm of poverty and injustice. In doing so, we can embrace a largely neglected piece of the heart of God. We will come to see that God passionately desires to do something about suffering in the world. Further, we will come to understand that He has invited us to be a part of His solution.

Through our acts of giving and assistance, our spirit will become attuned to the giving nature of God Himself. Our spiritual muscles will start to flex at the opportunity to give. We will no longer sit back and think, "I wonder if I should," as though our involvement is optional. We will become Pavlovian in our response to need. This is where God wants His children—He wants us to be so attuned to the suffering and pain of those around us that we respond to those needs without thinking. Giving to the needs of others, personally involving ourselves in the hopelessness of others, and diving into the misery of others in the name of Christ will become our second nature.

I've seen it happen countless times. Once a believer begins to give and pour out—once a believer has let go of the table and realized that not only can we balance on our own two feet, but we can walk . . . and not only can we walk, but we can actually run—everything changes.

WHAT ABOUT YOU?
HAVE YOU HELD ONTO THE TABLE LONG ENOUGH?

BEGINNING THE CONVERSATION

We have all come from very different backgrounds and very different life experiences. However, we have been brought by God to this moment in time with this book in our hands. God has a message for us regarding the way we live our lives. Get ready. We all have the opportunity to change in ways we can't yet imagine.

God's Word is far from silent in regard to these issues of social change. A tremendous amount of Scripture deals directly and specifically with the issues of poverty, injustice, and oppression. We're going to ask God some tough questions and get answers from Him in regard to our personal and corporate responsibility and opportunity to serve the poor, needy, widows, orphans, and aliens in Jesus' name. Be prepared. God will also ask tough questions of us. He will reveal areas of our heart that may be numb to the needs of those around us. He'll show each of us how He wants to involve us in His redemptive purposes for the world. But before we get there, let's just begin the conversation . . .

What should I bring before the Lord when I come to bow before God on high? Should I come before Him with burnt offerings, with year-old calves? Would the Lord be pleased with thousands of rams, or with ten thousand streams of oil? Should I give my firstborn for my transgression, the child of my body for my own sin? He has told you men what is good and what it is the Lord requires of you: Only to act justly, to love faithfulness, and to walk humbly with your God.

MICAH 6:6-8

BEGINNING THE CONVERSATION

A PROBLEM OF GEOGRAPHY

Americans live in a cocoon. This cocoon—made from the interwoven silks of economic, political, and ideological freedoms—effectively isolates us from connecting to (or fully understanding) the way in which the vast majority of people on this planet live. Here are some basic figures about life outside that cocoon: one third of the world—that's about 2 billion people, men, women and children—lives on less than $2 a day. That's $60 a month, $720 a year. Some of us spend that much on our cars each month (car payment, insurance, gas, etc.). That ought to be enough for us to realize there's a need.

> Do you agree that the U. S. lives in a cocoon, disconnected from the way the majority of the world lives?

> What societal elements or cultural perspectives do you believe contribute to this?

READ ROMANS 12
(yes, the whole thing).

Discuss or reflect upon Romans 12 focusing on how this chapter applies to our responsibility to meet the needs of the poor and oppressed around the world.

Our national economy and political freedoms are not the only things that separate us from understanding the way the majority of the world lives. We further separate ourselves as believers by refusing to educate ourselves on the more than 2000 verses in Scripture that clearly reveal the following perspectives: God's heart for the poor and oppressed, the true condition of our world, our responsibility and opportunity to spread the gospel by serving others in need, and the promise that God will empower His children to accomplish His goal of justice and mercy for all the world through his Son, Jesus Christ.

As Christ-followers in the United States, we tend to feed ravenously on every passage of Scripture that refers to the blessings we receive from God. While we gorge ourselves on those verses, we by and large give very little time to the many passages that speak of self-denial, service, sacrifice, suffering for the sake of the Gospel, and sharing in the misery of others.

As quick as I am to judge our actions as the people of God toward the poor and oppressed, (I put myself at the front of the line) I'm equally as quick to absolve most believers from blame for our collective inactivity. In fact, I'm surprised that we aren't even less aware than we currently are of the global crises that plague the majority of humankind. Given how sparingly Scripture regarding God's desire for our involvement in social action is preached, it is amazing that these issues are acknowledged at all. This is our first and greatest problem.

The cynical side of me thinks that social justice is not preached because people who are poor and oppressed can't do the two things that most preachers want everyone to do—attend their churches and give to their causes. Additionally, my own experience as a pastor helps me understand that these topics are not addressed from the pulpit because "service" and "sacrifice" in Jesus' name is difficult to teach in today's con-sumer-driven church culture.

In such a culture, the preacher is only as good as his last sermon. He is rated by the straw poll every week as people gather in the lobby to talk about their approval or disapproval of the day's message. In this environ-ment, many preachers stay away from the controversial subjects out of concern for reprisal in the form of lower attendance.

> Do you agree that our churches have become part of the entertainment culture of our world?

> How do you see your church in light of this charge?

Download the *Get Uncomfortable* playlist. Get the list from your group leader or at *www.threadsmedia. com/media.* Make it your "soundtrack" for this study.

Secondly, our churches aren't structured toward responding effectively to these global issues. Many churches in the U.S. today, especially the larger they get, become like country clubs rather than spiritual hospitals. Over time we become concerned about our needs more than the needs of others. We become so focused on our own personal or corporate growth and maturity in Christ that we miss out on countless opportunities to grow and mature through service and sacrifice.

Church slowly becomes all about us and little else. Reggie McNeal puts it this way: "[Church] members obviously have needs for pastoral care and spiritual growth. It is critical that these issues be addressed. However, I am raising the question of how many church activities for the already-saved are justified where there are people out there who have never been touched with Jesus' love? The answer is a whole lot less than we've got going on now." [1]

Finally, the Christian publishing industry produces next to no material on these subjects. I was challenged on this statement by a young man recently when he asked me, "How can you make such an over-arching statement about Christian publishing? What's your source for the assertions?"

Read each of the following passages and then write a one sentence summary after each summarizing the purpose of the passage:

JOHN 10:37
JOHN 13:17
JEREMIAH 22:16
JAMES 1:22
TITUS 1:16

I pulled out a couple of the most recent annual product catalogs that I get in the mail and said to the young man, "Come over here, and let's see what Christians are reading these days." The two catalogs we looked at happened to be from well known publishing houses. From a potpourri of just over 2000 books, these were the alarming results: 69 books were on the topics of evangelism and missions (about 3.4 percent), 18 books were dealing with the issues of generosity, compassion or charity (0.9 percent), and no books—none—dealing primarily with the topics of poverty, injustices, and the church's response. I could almost see the scales falling from the eyes of this young man as he asked, "What do we do about this?"

That's exactly the question I'm trying to answer, at least in part, with this study. These numbers show that many of us have turned the Bible into a self-help program rather than a life-long process of self-denial. If Christianity is really just a personal improvement program we would have to ignore what Jesus told His disciples: "If anyone wants to come with Me, he must deny himself, take up his cross, and follow Me. For whoever wants to save his life will lose it, but whoever loses his life because of Me will find it. What will it benefit a man if he gains the whole world yet loses his life? Or what will a man give in exchange for his life?" (Matthew 16:24-26).

So what do we do? We can sit idly by and hurl accusations at the preachers of our churches. We can judge the country-club mentality of some of our congregations. We can even blame the publishing industry for leading us in the direction of self-indulgence. What will come of that criticism? Nothing. The only option we have for profound change is to re-engage in the Word of God and then *do* what it says. We must take ownership of our faith. We must read, understand, and put into practice what our God truly wants from his children in relation to those who are in need.

Read James 1:22-25.

How does this passage describe a Christ-follower who knows what God expects but chooses not to respond?

IT'S ONLY THE BEGINNING

Over the next several weeks one thing is true: we have the potential to learn more about ourselves and about God through this study than we might expect. Through that process, we will be forced to compare our passions, values, and priorities with the passions, values, and priorities of God—and some of us will be found wanting. Some of us will see our true motivations exposed. But if we purposefully engage with this study and prayerfully consider God's character, the condition of our world, and our responsibility as members of the body of Christ, we will reap the rewards of a deeper and more intimate relationship with our Lord and a clarity of purpose that we may have never experienced. We'll see the world through spiritual lenses and begin to respond not with empathy or with apathy but with compassion that leads to action.

I can be so certain that we will each be transformed by our time with this study because it happened to me. A few years ago, I was one of the pastors who failed to teach about God's heart for the poor from the pulpit. I was a believer who contributed to the state of our publishing culture by purchasing and devouring Christian self-help books. I had little to no contact with those in need, and I was perfectly fine with that. My passion was evangelism—sharing God's love through Jesus with all who hadn't yet heard the gospel. I truly believed that I had been called by God to preach the gospel while others were gifted to serve the needy. And so I lived uncritically within the American cocoon.

Then I met Drew. Drew is a dear friend and a member of the church where I am pastor. Through a providential meeting with him just less than two years ago, God began the process of permanently altering my perspective on the Bible, evangelism, and the mission of the church. I began to study the Scripture through the eyes of my new friend. Months later, I remember confessing to Drew, "How have I completed five years of seminary, preached hundreds of sermons over the past 10 years, and missed over 2000, verses relating to God's heart for the poor?"

As a result of God's transforming love and nurturing through His Word as well as friendships with godly, selfless men like Drew, my heart has been changed to be in line with God's heart for those on this planet that are in greatest need.

Some of you will have a similar paradigm shift in relation to God's word. You'll see Scripture you know well and think, "He must be paraphrasing these passages." But you'll find as you search your own Bible trying to verify (or discount) what I've quoted in this study, that I've paraphrased nothing. I've not altered a single word of the text. Every passage quoted comes directly from the Bible. Believe me—I was as surprised as you may be. I continue to be surprised, and pleasantly so, at the grand plan God has for the world.

REDISCOVERING OUR CHRISTIAN HERITAGE
Most people don't put the study of history on their "things I like to do when I have some spare time" list. But for the purposes of gaining a better picture of all that we're going to learn, we must know what the church has done in the past. We must know the actions our Christian forefathers took before we were here.

The church was not always disconnected from the issues of poverty and injustice. History teaches us that many cultural changes were actually birthed in the church. Godly people like you and me saw a need in someone else's life, met it, and changed the fabric of the world around them. The abolition of slavery, prison reform, the establishment of hospitals and schools for the poor, women's rights, opposition to forced prostitution, the fight against child labor, and numerous other human rights and social justice issues can be largely credited to the faithful actions of passionate believers.

American historian Sydney Ahlstrom of Yale University explained that the great humanitarian movement of the 19th century was "incomprehensible" without the "collective conscious of evangelical America." The movement was built, he said, on "the Puritan's basic confidence that the world could be constrained and reformed in accordance with God's revealed will," and furthered by the revivalists' "demand for holiness [and their] calling for socially relevant Christian commitment as the proper sequel to conversion."[2] All these statements are true, and the church has, in fact, had an exemplary record in the past of being light in this dark world.

But the people of God have also been the catalyst for the Inquisition, defended slavery in the South from the pulpits of countless churches, and created the Ku Klux Klan. Each time such atrocities are committed, however, they can be patently dismissed as works done by those who have misused, misunderstood, or ignored the mandates of God. On the other hand, whenever even one believer chooses to "fear God and keep His commands" (Ecclesiastes 12:13) and does what is right in God's eyes, miraculous things happen. Many victories for the poor and suffering throughout history have been won through totally devoted Christ-followers.

In light of this cursory look at our activist heritage, the church's current silence and inactivity is a new phenomenon. This is particularly ironic because we have more information at our fingertips than at any other time in history, yet we struggle to take action on either a local or global scale.

Listen to "Our Place at the Table" before your group gets together to discuss this session. (Your group leader will send it to you via e-mail.) See if you agree about Todd and Drew's assessment of the state of the church.

Watch "More Than Stats" when your group meets. Is it uncomfortable for you to begin to see the true state of the world? Are you beginning to feel the weight of personal responsibility?

What are your reactions to this cursory look at the heritage of the church?

Do you agree that right now the church is generally silent and inactive on issues that were previously important to her?

A PRIMER ON THE ISSUES

Although I have put a tremendous amount of prayer and study into the development of this study, it is, at best, only a primer. This is only the start of a life long pursuit of God's purpose for your life in relation to His plan of salvation for the world through His Son. I doubt we can draw from this study a well-structured philosophy of ministry toward the needy and suffering of the world. I don't expect that.

What I do expect, is that after our time together you will have seen your personal responsibility as a child of God to respond to injustice in the world. I also expect the Lord to peak your interest and pierce your heart as He did mine so that this primer can be a launching pad for further exploration, learning, and action. My hope is that you take away from our time together with a deeper understanding of God's perspective on these important issues and that you have some idea how you may rightly apply what you've learned in your own church setting.

Many of you will go to a place you have not been. You will travel on roads that your feet have never touched. This foreign place that God wants to show you will, in time, become familiar, and eventually, you will call it home. In some ways, you will become like Paul who was on his way to Damascus when his life was changed by the "light of Christ." The scales fell from his eyes; a whole new world opened up to him. His perspective changed. Many of us have been living our Christian life with scales or faulty lenses covering our eyes that prevent us from seeing the world through the eyes of Jesus.

LETTING GO

Think for a moment how ridiculous it would be for me to ask my son, Parker, now that he's a runner, if he would like to spend a few days walking around the coffee table. He'd think I was punishing him for something he did. There's no way Parker would trade a Saturday of soccer, tree-climbing, bike-riding, and street football for a day of walking slowly around the coffee table. He used to love it, but that was before he realized that the world was so big and running was so exhilarating.

When we see what God has already "prepared ahead of time" (Ephesians 2:10) in relation to the needs of people in our world; when we see how big the world really is and how exhilarating it is to let go of the table and serve God with faith-filled abandon, we will never be satisfied merely attending Sunday services, Wednesday church dinners, weekly Bible studies, and annual Christmas gift drives. These will all continue to be good and meaningful parts of our Christian lives, but they will no longer be ends unto themselves. They will instead be places of empowerment and preparation for the great opportunities that lay before us. We will come to see that God has brought us together for such a time as this to change the world for what might be the last time.

What is Threads?

WE ARE A COMMUNITY OF PEOPLE WHO ARE PIECING THE CHRISTIAN LIFE TOGETHER, ONE EXPERIENCE AT A TIME.

We're rooted in Romans 12 and Colossians 3. We're serious about worshipping God with our lives. We want to understand the grace Jesus extended to us and act on it. We want community, need to worship, and aren't willing to hold back when the world needs help. We want to grow. We crave Bible study that raises questions, makes us think, and pushes us to own our faith. We're interested in friendships that are as strong as kinship—the kind of relationships that transform individuals into communities.

Our Bible studies are designed specifically for you, featuring flexible formats with engaging video, audio, and music. These discussion-driven studies intentionally foster group and individual connections and encourage practical application of Scripture. You'll find articles, staff and author blogs, podcasts, and lots of other great resources at:

threadsmedia.com

Stop by to join our online community — and come by to visit often!

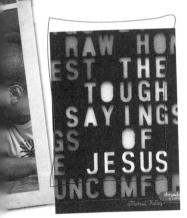

THE TOUGH SAYINGS OF JESUS
by Michael Kelley

This study explores four things Jesus said that are difficult to comprehend. Delving into the historical and cultural contexts of these Scriptures, the study focuses on sparking discussion and providing fresh insight, instead of pat answers. It will encourage you to embrace your doubts, and process through them, so that your faith can become deeper and stronger.

Michael Kelley is a writer and traveling communicator who speaks to students and young adults throughout the United States. Passionate about effectively communicating the fullness of the good news of Jesus, Michael previously served as the principle teacher for Refuge, a weekly worship event for young adults in Nashville, Tennessee. Visit him at www.michaelkelleyonline.com.

GET UNCOMFORTABLE:
SERVE THE POOR. STOP INJUSTICE.
CHANGE THE WORLD ... IN JESUS' NAME.
by Todd Phillips

Phillips guides you to understand how your faith in Christ and concern for the poor go hand-in-hand. As he examines God's character and perspective regarding poverty and injustice, he offers an understanding of what God calls you to do, along with practical ways to impact culture by caring for "the least of these."

Todd Phillips is the teaching pastor of Frontline, the young adult ministry of McLean Bible Church near Washington D.C. His passions are teaching the people of God and sharing the Gospel with those who aren't yet Christians. He is the author of Spiritual CPR: Reviving a Flat-lined Generation.

NO OTHER GODS:
CONFRONTING MODERN DAY IDOLS
by Kelly Minter

Do you worship the one true God, while also serving a bunch of smaller gods? No Other Gods: Confronting Our Modern-Day Idols is a Bible study for people seeking a place to openly talk about the little gods that take up our time, occupy space in our hearts, and impact our ability to serve. This study is designed to take place in a comfortable living room filled with friends, conversation, and good food—simple, yummy recipes included.

Kelly Minter is committed to using her talents and gifts to move people further along in their relationship with God. As a songwriter, worship leader, speaker, and author, Kelly travels extensively across the country. Find out more about the ministry of Kelly Minter at www.kellyminter.com.

**For full details on all of Threads'
studies, visit www.threadsmedia.com.**

group contact information

Name _____ Number _____
E-mail _____

Name _____ Number _____
E-mail _____

Name _____ Number _____
E-mail _____

Name _____ Number _____
E-mail _____

Name _____ Number _____
E-mail _____

Name _____ Number _____
E-mail _____

Name _____ Number _____
E-mail _____

Name _____ Number _____
E-mail _____

Name _____ Number _____
E-mail _____

Name _____ Number _____
E-mail _____

Name _____ Number _____
E-mail _____